WHITE JUSTICE IN ARIZONA

WHITE JUSTICE IN ARIZONA

Apache Murder Trials in the Nineteenth Century

CLARE V. MCKANNA JR.

Texas Tech University Press

This book is typeset in Sabon. The paper used in this book meets the minimum requirements of ANSI/NISO Z39.48-1992 (R1997).

Library of Congress Cataloging-in-Publication Data
McKanna, Clare V. (Clare Vernon), 1935-
  White justice in Arizona : Apache murder trials in the nineteenth century / Clare V. McKanna, Jr.
      p.   cm.
  Includes bibliographical references and index.
  ISBN 0-89672-554-5 (cloth : alk. paper) — ISBN 0-89672-555-3 (pbk. : alk. paper)
1. Apache Indians—Arizona. 2. Apache Indians—Government relations—Arizona.
3. Trials (Murder)—Arizona. I. Title.
E99.A6M427 2005
323.1197'250791'09034—dc22   2005003976

ISBN 13 978-89672-554-6

05 06 07 08 09 10 11 12 13 / 9 8 7 6 5 4 3 2 1

Printed in the United States of America

Texas Tech University Press
Box 41037
Lubbock, Texas 79409-1037 USA
800.832.4042
ttup@ttu.edu
www.ttup.ttu.edu

*For the Apaches and all Native Americans
who suffered great injustice in the Liminal World,
betwixt and between*

CONTENTS

ILLUSTRATIONS

PREFACE

THIS BOOK had its genesis during a National Endowment for the Humanities summer seminar, in 1988, held in Tucson, Arizona. Professor Roger Nichols, of the University of Arizona, had graciously invited me to attend his colloquium examining "New Directions in Native American History." My main research goal at the seminar focused on examining homicide cases from six Arizona counties to determine whether ethnic minorities received fair treatment in the criminal justice systems. In late August, I had finally achieved my main goal of researching the Arizona State Archives. As I sat there on my last day waiting for records to be paged up, out of curiosity I decided to do some "fishing" through a few archival guides. I turned to the nineteenth-century records for the Arizona Territorial Supreme Court and began to browse. Suddenly, I noticed a series of homicide cases with Apache names that had been appealed in 1888. The court had reversed eleven cases and sent them back to the counties of origin for retrial. After I asked the archivist to page them he suggested using the microfilm, but I firmly insisted on looking at the case files, and he relented. My first look at these court cases left me stunned; I had, indeed, found a treasure of information about how the Arizona territorial criminal justice system treated Apache defendants. All of the trial transcripts in these files proved to be short, averaging around twenty-five to thirty pages, and yet all of the defendants had been convicted in the U.S. District Courts, Arizona Territory. Since these were murder cases that could end with the death penalty, I quickly realized that these stories had to be told; they were crying for an audience, and I decided that it would be my backup project. I copied the Gonshayee case and a list of the other ten cases. Although delayed for several years, this project was the beginning of a remarkable journey that would tell the stories of Captain Jack, Gonshayee, Apache Kid, Nahdeizaz, and another, later homicide case in 1890 involving Batdish and three other defendants. This, then, is their story.

ACKNOWLEDGMENTS

I WISH TO THANK Professor Roger Cunniff, Department of History, and Clare Colquitt, Department of Comparative Literature and English, San Diego State University; both are good friends and honest critics. Judith Keeling, editor in chief, Texas Tech University Press, provided moral support throughout the review process, and I also wish to thank Professor Alwyn Barr and the two anonymous reviewers who offered much-needed criticism that helped to shape the final manuscript.

A special thanks to Melodie Tune, graphic artist, Instructional Technology Services, San Diego State University, for designing and completing the crime scene maps and illustrations. I would like to acknowledge archivists David H. Hoober, Jean Nudd, Wendi Goen, and Nancy Sawyer at the Arizona State Archives, Phoenix, who provided invaluable assistance in locating court records. I also appreciated the aide of Alan Ferg, archivist, Arizona State Museum, who graciously allowed me to research in the Grenville Goodwin Collection. The archivists of the Old Military Records, National Archives, also provided much-needed help by locating and copying the Apache Kid Court-Martial file. Finally, a special thanks to the College of Arts and Letters, San Diego State University, for funding additional research in the summer of 2000.

WHITE JUSTICE IN ARIZONA

WHITE MAN'S LAW

There is one, and only one, thing in modern society
more hideous than crime—namely, repressive justice.

SIMONE WEIL,

"Human Personality," *La Table Ronde,* 1950

FRENCH PHILOSOPHER Simone Weil understood well the danger that existed when justice became perverted by the state. On occasion we need to reflect upon injustices committed in the past that are disguised as justice. The separation of powers in the U.S. Constitution was developed specifically to safeguard such basic rights. It is important to remember that if you are not treated fairly in the courts there is no recourse, and therefore, there is no justice. Unfair treatment is exactly what happened to indigenous peoples not only in Arizona Territory but also throughout the United States. Beginning in the seventeenth and continuing through the nineteenth century, British and American legal authorities failed to protect the legal rights of Pequot, Ojibwa, Cree, Dakota, and, in this study, Apache defendants. The four Apache trials that follow provide a sad commentary on the state of justice, and they certainly do not reflect the basic tenets of a democratic society. Placing the Apache defendants on trial in an open court might suggest fairness, but it was not. In 1980, in a dissenting opinion on a murder conviction of Elmer "Geronimo" Pratt, in the court of appeals in California, Justice George William Dunn suggested: "A trial which is not fundamentally fair is no trial at all. It is a non sequitur to argue that a defendant is obviously guilty if it is an established fact that the defendant was not afforded a fair trial."[1] That is precisely what happened to these Apache defendants.

This is a discussion of the American legal tradition and its application to an Apache culture that lived by a very different social and legal code. The harsh enforcement of the white man's rules of law over all ethnic groups in Arizona Territory provides ample evidence of injustice. Unfortunately, we know little of the Apache social forces and legal customs that enabled them to sustain a civil society for hundreds of years before the Europeans entered their world. Although the Apache did not develop a written history of this system, there is little doubt that they created and modified a legal culture that worked for them. They were overwhelmed by white outsiders who conquered them; forced them off their land; ignored their civilization, social customs, and methods of maintaining social control over their people; and displayed a great deal of hatred toward them. There are major gaps in our knowledge of the treatment of Native Americans in our criminal justice systems because most historians, except for Sidney Harring, Yasuhide Kawashima, and a few others, have ignored them. Consequently, this study is an attempt to articulate what happened to Apache defendants accused of murder and to evaluate how they fared in Arizona's territorial courts and, to a lesser extent, in the U.S. Supreme Court. By no means is this a definitive legal history about the treatment of the Apache in Arizona Territory; but, hopefully, it is the beginning of a dialogue on the handling of America's indigenous population under the control of U.S. federal, state, and county criminal justice systems. In analyzing the research on this legal history it should be understood that most of the documents and sources reflect a white perspective. That places a heavy burden upon the author to ensure that Apache legal history and social customs, and the treatment of Apaches by white authorities, become a part of this discussion and to give them a voice in this drama, no matter how small. The main story, however, is the legal methods used by white society to enforce its will on the Apache and the ultimate consequences of these methods. As will be seen, similar patterns were established and used early in British and American history.

INDIANS AND THE BRITISH-AMERICAN LEGAL TRADITION

British legal doctrine, based upon English common law, the infamous "bloody codes" with over two hundred capital offenses and a severe, retributive type of punishment, was transported to the colonies in the early seventeenth century. In colonial America this legal tradition continued into the late nineteenth century. In New England, Puritan officials prosecuted Pequots and other Indians for murder during times of conflict, such as the King Philip's War. In 1675 magistrates brought charges against "Little John" for killing a white citizen in Lancaster. More Native Americans were accused of murder the following year. On September 13, 1676, Judge Samuel Sewall noted in his diary the execution of Indians who had been convicted of murder: "The after part of the day very rainy. There were eight Indians shot to death on the Common, upon Wind-mill hill." It should be noted that despite the intense warfare, the Pequot defendants were not considered to be prisoners of war. One historian noted that there were more Indians convicted and executed but that their exact numbers "cannot be determined." Further research has found six other executions of Native Americans in 1675; five were hanged and one was shot.[2]

Historian Yasuhide Kawashima provides a more detailed

discussion of how the Puritans treated local Indians accused of murder and manslaughter. Apparently, there was relatively little Indian crime even during periods of war, such as Queen Anne's War, yet "the rate of convictions went up in times of political conflict and stress." In general, Puritan authorities tried to treat all of their subjects fairly, which included guaranteeing "fundamental procedural rights, such as trial by jury and right of appeal" to Native Americans as well as whites.[3] Not surprisingly Puritans considered Indian killings of whites to be more serious than whites killing Indians. On October 21, 1696, a "special Court of Oyer and Terminer" tried four Mohawks accused of killing one white male near Hatfield. The jury found all four guilty and sentenced them to death. They were shot two days later. Kawashima discovered that sometimes "whites accused of murdering natives either received lighter penalties" or "escaped punishment altogether." For example, in 1750, several white men attacked and killed a friendly Penobscot and wounded others while they were sleeping. Eventually captured, the white men were tried while several Penobscot tribal members watched. They were "astonished as the jury refused to convict" the white defendants during a trial that included strong evidence of their guilt. Few Indians were charged with manslaughter against whites, suggesting that white juries "had come to regard all Indian killings of whites as murder."[4]

Although not common, a few Native Americans charged with raping white women received death sentences. In an unusual case in 1674, a jury of "six Englishmen and six Indians" convicted and sentenced to death an Indian named Tom for raping a white woman. Eight years later, in another case involving rape, the legal authorities ordered Sam, the condemned prisoner, to be "severely whipped and then banished from the colony." Oddly enough, the condemned received a reduced sentence because the magistrates reasoned that Sam "was but an Indian." In 1740, a jury indicted, tried, and sentenced to death another Indian in York County; he was executed three weeks later.[5] Kawashima discovered eight murder cases with Indians killing whites and ten cases where they killed fellow tribesmen in five Massachusetts counties from 1689 to 1763. An additional eight Indian defendants were convicted of manslaughter against other Indians.[6] The author concluded that the Puritan judicial system "generally prevented arbitrariness" when dealing with Indians accused of crimes. It was also apparent that "although the courts probably sensed the cultural differences between the two races . . . few records show that the courts ever took full consideration of the Indian law." Racial "prejudice, fear, [and] condescension" coupled with dramatic cultural differences sometimes led "to instances of harsh treatment." Finally, it was clear that Puritan authorities administered their criminal justice system in order to "extract social conformity" among all of its subjects, white, black, and Indian.[7]

While examining the treatment of the indigenous population in Canada, Sidney Harring discovered that in the late eighteenth and early nineteenth centuries white settlers committed numerous depredations against Indians that included killings. Soldiers from Kingston, Ontario, killed Chief Snake in 1792 and, four years later, four soldiers in York beat to death Chief Wabakinine. "The killers of Chief Snake were acquitted," and no criminal charges were filed in the Wabakinine case. The white settlers virtually got away with murder.[8] In 1822, legal authorities in Amherstburg prosecuted Shawanakiskie, an Ottawa, for killing an Indian woman. Defense counsel argued to no avail that by tribal custom "he had avenged the murder of a parent, a justifiable killing under tribal law" and that treaties protected this indigenous practice. Nevertheless, a jury convicted and sentenced him to death.[9]

Occasionally Canadian legal authorities had to deal with a variety of Native American traditions involving evil spirits and witches that ran counter to white cultural values. Harring examined seven cases of murder or manslaughter involving "'wendigo' killings." *Wendigos* were evil spirits and, real or imagined, proved to be a threatening force to the Ojibwa, who believed they had been cursed. On December 3, 1896, legal authorities at Sabascon, near Lake of the Woods, brought murder charges against Machekequonabe. The defendant, and seven other Ojibwa guarding their village against spiritual threats, had seen signs of wendigo activity nearby. A. S. Winks, of Port Arthur, hired by the Indian Department to represent Machekequonabe against charges of murder, failed to adequately defend his client. "The entire case was based totally on the testimony of one man, Wasawpscopinesse, and, judging from the length of the transcript [twelve pages], took only a few hours." The court convicted the defendant of murder but spared him from the death penalty.[10]

In another wendigo case, legal authorities quickly convicted Joseph Fiddler of murder and sentenced him to death. With the entire trial lasting less than one day, these two cases parallel similar patterns of the prosecution of California Indian homicide cases.[11] Harring concludes that the Canadian legal authorities decided to make a statement that those accused of wendigo killings would be harshly dealt with.[12] Further, Harring determines that Canadian authorities apparently had no intention of accommodating "the tribes by attempting to incorporate the honestly held beliefs of Indians into their traditional common law defences. However, this was beyond colonial jurisprudence."[13]

As white settlers began to push into the western prairies of Canada, the government established the North-West Mounted Police [NWMP], led by officers who were appointed as magistrates to maintain order and deal with crime. Harring notes that the NWMP "was a self-contained legal institution" whose officers "arrested, prosecuted, judged, and jailed offenders under their jurisdiction."[14] Some Mounty officers were appointed as justices of the peace, and they were given the authority to try any law violators. In the 1880s, during the Riel rebellion, Canadian authorities charged numerous Indians with treason and murder. They tried, convicted, and sentenced forty Cree and Métis to Stony Mountain Prison, and eight were hanged for murder. All-white, male juries seeking retribution for the killing of white settlers often convicted the defendants regardless of the evidence. Harring concludes that "the quality of justice rendered was a travesty."[15] Like the Ojibwa wendigo murder cases, these Cree prosecutions were also very short trials that often lasted less than a day. In Regina, Saskatchewan, authorities prosecuted "Bad Arrow, Miserable Man, Walking the Sky, Little Bear, Iron Body," all Cree, for murder. With partisan judges and no legal counsel (the government refused to provide lawyers), the outcome of the trial was predictable: they were convicted and sentenced to death. A large crowd attended the executions, and "the warriors sang their death chants" before the hanging. Black caps were put over the heads of all eight of the condemned executed at Battleford.[16] Harring suggests that at its best the NWMP "constituted a liberal, authoritarian, and paternalistic legal institution," but at its worst, it "was a racist and paramilitary organization." As the NWMP extended Canadian legal powers into the west, its "officers served as police, prosecutor, judge, jury, and executioner."[17] Unfortunately, they seldom considered fairly the needs and rights of Canada's indigenous population, who suffered under such legal tyranny.

Similar patterns of British subjects abusing indigenous peoples have been discovered in Australia, where whites killed aboriginal peoples with virtual impunity. In one case, where eleven white defendants were charged with killing twenty-eight Ab-origines, an all-white, male jury found them not guilty in "only fifteen minutes." During the 1830s and 1840s, in New South Wales, Australia, there were at least thirteen cases where Ab-origines convicted of killing whites were sentenced to death. Others who received long prison sentences usually died very quickly after being incarcerated.[18] The British treatment of indigenous defendants provides a thread of history that extends into the nineteenth-century American West, where authorities continued this long tradition of failing to protect the rights of indigenous populations.

U.S. LEGAL TRADITION AT MANKATO, 1862

During the nineteenth century, after developing reservations to control Native Americans, the U.S. government frequently failed to fulfill its treaty-bound obligations to properly take care of its wards. In Minnesota, the Dakota were placed on a strip of land about twenty miles wide that stretched from north to southeast for about ninety miles along the Minnesota River from Appleton to a few miles from New Ulm. Experiencing dif-ficulty surviving on this small reservation and facing often late arriving annuities from the government, the Dakota grew rest-less in the summer of 1862. Further complicating the situation, food could have been released by the traders but, following governmental policies that tended to be bureaucratic, the traders refused to give them food until the annuities arrived. Andrew Myrick, a trader, allegedly said, "So far as I am con-cerned, if they are hungry, let them eat grass."[19] In mid-August a small hunting party of Dakota were returning home without game and were angry. As they passed a farm they attacked and "killed five American settlers on two homesteads in Acton, Minnesota."[20] This event quickly escalated into a full-fledged war led by Little Crow and other Dakota chiefs. By mid-September, when the war ended, it had cost the lives of about 358 settlers, approximately 106 soldiers and armed settlers, an estimated 29 Dakota soldiers, and an unknown number of Dakota men, women, and children. Eventually, an estimated twelve hundred Dakota surrendered to General Henry Sibley.[21]

During the war against the Dakota, some white combatants, seeking to gain revenge for their battle losses, "scalped dead Indians." An angry Sibley stated that the defeated should "not be subjected to indignities by civilized and Christian men."[22] Sibley, however, had no qualms about dealing harshly with the captured Dakota who were brought before a military tribunal. Even though he had no legal authority, Sibley's intentions were "to execute promptly all the men found guilty" by the tribunal.[23] General John Pope, his superior, expressed his hatred for the Dakota and, on October 1, sent a letter to Sibley stating that he "approve[d] of executing the Indians who have been concerned in these outrages."[24] General Pope advised Sibley that now was the time to deal ruthlessly with the Dakota, and if any left the reservation, "that all the soldiers have orders to shoot them"; he also stated that the settlers should do the same.[25] Sibley, along with most Minnesota settlers, shared a mutual hatred for the Dakota, and many would have been content with exterminating all of them. Numerous newspapers in Mankato, Minnesota, and other towns ran banner headlines and editorials calling for their utter destruction. The Mankato *Independent* editor called "for the extermination of Indians" accused of murders and acts of war during the uprising.[26]

General Sibley appointed five military officers, ranking from colonel to lieutenant, to try the Dakota prisoners.[27] All of them had "fought in the battles" to suppress the Dakota uprising, and law professor Carol Chomsky astutely observes that "it is inconceivable that they came to their task with open minds."[28]

Lieutenant Rollin C. Olin, just twenty-one, with "no legal training," received the assignment as judge advocate to preside over the military court. The first problem facing the tribunal: with what crimes should the Dakota defendants be charged? In times of war, and this one had all the earmarks for it, prisoners were treated as prisoners of war. The tribunal, however, chose to strip them of such rights and decided to charge them as common criminals who had committed acts of "murder, rape, and robbery." Sibley, in a letter to General Pope, suggested that "the horrible massacres of women and children . . . call for punishment beyond human power to inflict." He claimed that they should "be treated as maniacs and wild beasts."[29] With such inflammatory statements from Sibley, along with the attitudes shared by the military tribunal, it is not surprising that the defendants failed to receive fair trials or justice. Several factors illuminate the failure to protect the Dakota defendants' legal rights. For example, they were denied legal counsel; the trials were conducted in English, which often prevented the defendants from understanding the charges filed against them; they were not tried as prisoners of war; and they were railroaded through the military legal process very quickly.[30] These factors ensured that the tribunal would have incredibly high conviction rates.

The trials of 392 Dakota defendants were conducted with great haste, many taking less than five minutes for the tribunal to reach a verdict. Within a short period of time, then, the tribunal convicted 323 defendants and sentenced 303 to death by hanging. Chomsky's research revealed that forty-two cases were tried on a single day. Minnesota Reverend J. P. Williamson claimed that the "400 trials have been tried in less time than is general[ly] taken in our courts with the trial of a single murderer."[31] General Sibley, with the support of General Pope and virtually the entire white population of Minnesota, wanted to execute all of the 303 condemned prisoners; however, he did not have the legal authority.

President Abraham Lincoln received the unenviable task of determining which of the 303 condemned would be executed. The events in Minnesota had caught him at a difficult time; the Civil War was going badly and he had just lost a son. Various forces began to pressure him to act quickly; he "received three hundred letters a day," many calling for him to execute every one of the prisoners.[32] Lincoln would not be stampeded into making his decision despite the intense pressure. One historian suggested that "Lincoln would not be swayed by the mob's demands—at least not all of them."[33] First, Lincoln ordered Sibley to forward full transcripts of all condemned prisoners so that he could assess them in order to make his decisions. Then the president assigned two aides to examine them and make recommendations based upon the seriousness of the charges. After an agonizing session examining the recommendations of his aides, Lincoln finally sent a message to Sibley ordering him to execute thirty-nine of the condemned on December 19.

Because of the delay in delivering the message, Sibley had to inform the president that he could not execute them until December 26. One reason for the delay was that the military officers in charge could not find enough rope in Mankato, Minnesota, the site of the executions, to hang all of the prisoners.[34] Further, the military authorities had to construct a huge scaffold that would enable them to hang all of the condemned at the same time. Finally, on December 26, a cold, wet, wintry day, approximately four thousand people crowded into the square in Mankato to watch the hangings. At 10 a.m., as the soldiers led the Dakota warriors to the scaffold, they began to sing their death songs. They mounted the platform, had the ropes adjusted around their necks, had white hoods placed over their heads, and, at the third strike of the drum, William Duley used an axe to cut a single rope that opened thirty-eight trap doors. The men all dropped at the same time and were "left dangling between heaven and earth." At first the crowd cheered, then fell silent.[35]

One of the most remarkable things about the Mankato, Minnesota, executions was the sheer magnitude and the haste of the prosecution to gain convictions of the accused Dakota prisoners. This mass execution is unparalleled in the history of criminal justice in the United States. No American could honestly call it justice—it was retribution against the killing of white settlers and soldiers. As stated earlier, there were forty-two trials held on a single day. Assuming the tribunal had an eight-hour session, which is unlikely, that would allow a little longer than eleven minutes per defendant. Chomsky examined the arraignment page of the transcripts and discovered that, in many of them, "the page appears to have been prepared in advance . . . with blank spaces for name and date to be added at the trial."[36] All the military officers had to do was fill in the blanks. Obviously this aided them in quickly dispatching with each defendant; there is no indication of any attempts to be impartial and fair in their final judgment. Chomsky concludes that "the trials and executions became an exercise of power, not law."[37] And these executions did not placate the Minnesota populace, who held tremendous hatred toward the Dakota and other Indians. For example, by the summer of 1863, a year after the Dakota war, "Minnesota had a $200 bounty on Dakota scalps." No doubt it became unsafe for the Dakota to travel around Minnesota. Eventually, they were removed to Crow Creek in South Dakota.[38]

This discussion of criminal justice makes it clear that the British-American legal tradition had a long history of failing to protect the rights of Native Americans in the courts. Beginning with the Puritans in New England, these injustices were paralleled by similar legal tactics in Canada, Australia, and the

western United States and continued right through the nineteenth century. How this distorted legal culture impacted
Apache defendants accused of murder in Arizona Territory, is
the main focus of this book. We need to closely examine and
carefully evaluate how and why this legal system continued
such unjust policies against the Apaches and, hopefully, we may
gain a better understanding of the weaknesses in our criminal
justice systems. This discussion should make us more aware of
the policies of racial discrimination that still plague our criminal justice system today.

THE APACHE HOMICIDE CASES

The four case studies presented here provide an opportunity to
examine and critique the operation of the criminal justice
system in Arizona Territory in the late nineteenth century,
during a time period when the dominant white culture regarded
all Native Americans, but especially Apaches, as "savages."
More specifically, these cases provide a lens through which to
observe the treatment of Apache defendants accused of committing homicides. Each case, of course, is unique; these four
murder trials provide very different circumstances but conclude
with similar results.

Blood feuds, or vendettas, were common among the
Apaches and other Native Americans. Usually they tried to
settle these disputes through negotiations between the two families or bands. Normally a payment in horses, blankets, and
other goods would be satisfactory; however, if they could not
agree, the aggrieved party virtually had the right to kill a
member of the rival band. The first chapter of this book examines Apache legal customs, the tradition of blood feuds with
Casadora's band, the Arizona territorial criminal justice system,
Captain Jack's trial, the appeal to the U.S. Supreme Court, and
the consequences for the defendants. This case study offers

insights into the administration of justice in Arizona Territory and reveals that, on occasion, justice could be gained, at least by one Apache defendant.

For generations the Apaches had participated in raiding parties in search of horses and other livestock throughout what became Arizona Territory. The second chapter discusses Apache social traditions such as *tiswin* drinking parties, the story of Apache Kid's revenge against a rival band member for killing his father, and the "last raid" of Kid along with Gonshayee's band. This case study also analyzes the court-martial of Kid for mutiny, the murder trial of Gonshayee, a brief discussion of *Ex Parte Crow Dog* and *Ex Parte Gonshayee* (U.S. Supreme Court cases), and, finally, Gonshayee's conviction in his second trial. This murder case provides insights into Apache behavior that sometimes led to raids in the nineteenth century; however, that lifestyle would no longer be tolerated under territorial law, and the consequences for Apache defendants accused of killing white victims were predictably severe.

In the third case study we turn to Nahdeizaz and the treatment of young Apaches who had been sent to "away school" during the nineteenth century. Usually they attended the schools for several years before returning to their homes. Upon their return they found themselves accepted neither by their band members nor by the white community that controlled their destiny. The Indian agent sent Nahdeizaz to Carlisle Indian School, where he suffered away school trauma: the loss of family ties, denial of spiritual rituals and language, and, of course, the loss of his tribal identity. This case examines the methods of Captain Richard Henry Pratt, the superintendent of the Carlisle school; the plight of the "returned students"; and the social conditions in San Carlos, Arizona. It will also include a brief discussion of the killing of Lieutenant Seward Mott, Nahdeizaz's trial, and the final results. This chapter reveals the destructive results of the away school concept that alienated young students and sometimes caused them to commit acts of violence. Sadly, this was Lieutenant Mott's first assignment out of West Point, and his brief tenure (three months) at San Carlos proved to be tragic for himself and Nahdeizaz.

The fourth case offers a window of opportunity to examine the trial of Batdish, Bakelcle, Guadalupe, and Natsin, Apache defendants accused of murdering a white man on Baker's Mountain in the rugged Sierra Ancha range west of San Carlos. Similar to the other cases, the defendants received court-appointed attorneys, and consequently, they were placed at a great disadvantage in the criminal justice system. This chapter opens with a brief description of the killing, followed by a discussion of homicide investigatory practices in the nineteenth century, the use of Apache scouts, their tracking methods, and the trailing of the killers. The chapter concludes with an examination of the prosecution and defense cases, the guilty verdict, the appeal to the Supreme Court of Arizona Territory, and the results of the appeal. In this case, the circumstantial evidence proved to be weak and unconvincing; the trail of the killers neither crossed nor converged with that of the defendants. Al Sieber, chief of scouts, and his Apache scouts believed the defendants were innocent. The feeble defense given the Apache defendants, an all-white jury, and a white victim help to explain the final verdict. The Batdish case study provides a natural comparison with the 1892 trial of José Gabriel, in San Diego, California; both reveal examples of injustice in white-controlled criminal justice systems.[39]

The Epilogue briefly compares Apache and white conviction rates in six Arizona Territory counties and discusses the double standard of justice: white prosecutors sought the death penalty when an Apache murdered a white; whites who killed Apaches or other Indians, by contrast, were rarely punished. Prosecutors

Map of Arizona showing San Carlos Reservation in the
nineteenth century. *Courtesy of Melodie Tune, graphic artist,
Instructional Technology Services, San Diego State University.*

were, however, more lenient when the victims of Apache violence were other Apaches, especially females. For Apaches,
being sent to prison meant hard time, and many died of consumption in federal and state prisons.[40] Finally, there is a brief
examination of the devastating consequences for the defendants
in these case studies.

CHAPTER 1

CAPTAIN JACK'S "VENDETTA"

*"It was customary among his people that where an Indian
had killed in order to avenge him, that relatives of the
Indian were justified in killing one of the other
band in satisfaction."*
COLONEL SIMON SNYDER,
U.S. v. Captain Jack, May 1888

DURING the nineteenth century the white-dominated criminal
justice system in Arizona Territory placed Apache defendants
accused of murder at risk. Instead of being held to the social
behavior standards of their peers, now they would be judged by
an alien system that seemed incomprehensible. Because of sharp
cultural contrasts, Apaches perceived homicide very differently
than whites. Apache band chiefs held only nominal power over
their clan members and could not always dictate or control
their behavior. Consequently, Apaches developed social control
mechanisms that relegated homicide punishment to the family
or the clan.

By 1887, most of the Western Apaches were confined to San
Carlos Reservation without a substitute for their old lifestyle of
raiding for cattle and horses. Captain Jack, leader of a Pinal
Apache band (designated SC by the U.S. government), was

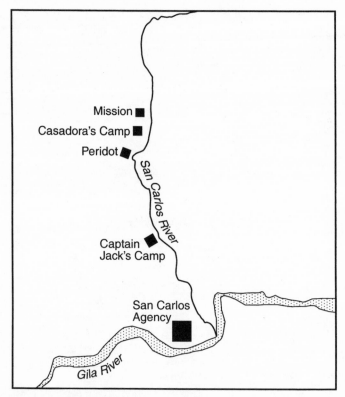

Map of Old San Carlos showing the camps of Captain Jack and
Casadora, 1887. *Courtesy of Melodie Tune, graphic artist, Instructional
Technology Services, San Diego State University*

living four miles north of the San Carlos agency along the San
Carlos River. Casadora, the leader of a San Carlos band (designated SJ), lived about four miles farther north, and, from time
to time, they would pass by the SC band camp on their way to
the agency; because of insults, hostility between these rival
groups began to fester. In early 1888, one or more members of
Casadora's clan killed two members of Captain Jack's band
and, a few months later, killed another man. Unable to gain
satisfaction for these killings, Captain Jack began to worry
that he might be attacked again by his rival. On April 10,

1888, Casadora and several of his band, armed with rifles, approached Captain Jack's camp. Fearful of an attack, members of Captain Jack's band shot and killed two members of Casadora's band. Under the Major Crimes Act of 1885, U.S. Army officers could no longer allow Apaches to settle their disputes by tribal means. It was now up to the legal authorities at San Carlos to enforce laws. Therefore, they arrested the suspects. These two killings provide an opportunity to explore Apache blood feuds and how, in this case, they were resolved by an Arizona territorial criminal justice system that failed to understand band rivalries and their consequences.

APACHE LEGAL TRADITION

William Seagle, in his discussion of Indian legal traditions, suggests that "some very primitive societies . . . discovered methods of mitigating the blood-feud" without established courts.[1] However, E. Adamson Hoebel claims that the concept of courts as defined by modern jurisprudence was not the real issue in assessing Native American legal tradition. Hoebel suggests that "the really fundamental *sine qua non* of law in any society— primitive or civilized—is the legitimate use of physical coercion by a socially authorized agent."[2] Similarly, A. R. Radcliffe-Brown views law as "the maintenance or establishment of social order . . . by the exercise of coercive authority through the use, or the possibility of use, of physical force."[3] Hoebel ultimately concludes that law may be defined in these terms: "*A social norm is legal if its neglect or infraction is regularly met, in threat or in fact, by the application of physical force by an individual or group possessing the socially recognized privilege of so acting.*"[4] Viewing law within this context aids in understanding Native American methods of controlling homicide.

Notably, there was no unanimity among Native American

tribes on the classification and punishment of homicide. The Cheyenne viewed homicide as a "sin." The tribal council held the ultimate authority in murder cases, and even they could not condemn the perpetrator to death. "The solution was exile, and this was the sentence. Thus homicide was made a crime against the people."[5] After banishing the offender, the Cheyenne performed the ritual of "Renewal of the Medicine Arrows" to purge them from any bad medicine brought on by the murder of a Cheyenne. After leaving the camp, the perpetrator continued his or her life in another area. The Cheyenne, however, believed in redemption and, if the kin of the victim did not object, the killer could eventually return to the camp. Intratribal homicide was rare among the Cheyenne; George Bird Grinnell, a naturalist who also studied Native American culture, believed that sixteen cases occurred between 1835 and 1879. With an estimated population of 8,500, that would be approximately four homicides per 100,000 population per year, a low rate compared to white-dominated areas of the American West.[6]

John Phillip Reid claims that the Cherokee knew the law of homicide well, that "it was ingrained in his legal consciousness, the bone and marrow of his social existence." It was the "foundation of most primitive legal systems" and was necessary for maintaining the social structure of Native American societies. Reid further notes that "talionic justice was by no means an institution of uniform application."[7] There was a wide variety of methods to deal with homicide. Plains Indians used the peace pipe as a means of persuasion to stop blood feuds. The Iroquois would convene a council to deal with homicides with the purpose of forestalling the "retaliatory killing."[8] The variety of methods available to deal with homicide is striking and not always conducive to mitigation. For example, the Comanche believed that a man had the right to kill his wife "with or without good cause," and it was not considered to be murder.

To the Comanche, "homicide was not legally a tribal or public affair." It was a quarrel for the family to resolve, and tribal government had no right to interfere.[9]

The Western Apaches perceived homicide in a manner somewhat similar to that of the Comanche. Apache leadership did not possess a tribal council tradition of strong central power; instead, Apache band or clan chiefs often could not dictate or control clan behavior. Leaders were respected for their power and leadership, but if they did not satisfy the majority, they could be quickly deposed.[10] This diffuse leadership style may explain why the Western Apaches developed social control mechanisms that paralleled the Comanche concept of it being a "family matter." With the Apaches, however, the whole clan acted as the "family." Apaches believed that a man had the right to cut off his wife's nose if she had been unfaithful, and it was acceptable to kill her as well. If someone raped his wife, the husband "would attempt to kill the other man, and in doing so, public sentiment . . . would be with him."[11] If someone accidentally killed another, or killed in anger, it was common to pay atonement. If accepted by the aggrieved party, the issue could be resolved. In such cases, close blood relatives of the injured party demanded and accepted such payments. If the atonement was insufficient or if the killing was accompanied by great anger, the victim's family could kill the murderer.

APACHE FEUDS

Interband feuds were frequent within Western Apache culture and created a certain amount of instability. Apaches tended to hold grudges and believed in "getting even." Once the loss became "equal," the feud could end, but in some cases the feuds escalated. In many ways Apache social controls for homicide parallel the feuding tradition prevalent within Mediterranean societies such as in Sicily, Sardinia, Corsica, Italy, and Montenegro.[12] Among the Apaches, the wronged party, whether it be homicide, wife rape, or just an insult, might ambush the perpetrator without warning. Homicides were often committed "during or following drinking parties" where, under the influence of tiswin, old grudges might be recalled and "settled."[13] On numerous occasions, the Indian agent at San Carlos complained of the nature of these drunken bouts. In 1889, Captain John L. Bullis, Indian agent, admitted that tiswin drinking bouts continued to plague the reservation and usually ended in the killing of one or more participants.[14]

Grenville Goodwin reports that a significant number of homicides involving tiswin had been committed during the late nineteenth century. An informant told Goodwin that "whenever one man had killed another, he continually carries weapons with him," hoping to prevent an ambush. Goodwin observes that "too much stress cannot be placed on the clan nature of feuds. The opposing party was not spoken of as the enemy of the family . . . but as the enemy of the clan."[15] His informants recounted several revenge homicides that dramatically escalated out of control. According to Anna Price, an Apache informant, a killing among the White Mountain Apaches in 1850 led to a virtual bloodbath. A group of Apaches participated in a game of hoop-and-pole and soon began to quarrel. One man fatally stabbed another, jumped on his horse, and galloped away. In a running battle he killed one of his pursuers. Within a few minutes he had killed four. In the ensuing melee "twenty-two men were killed."[16] Anna Price's father returned from a hunting trip, and, after hearing of the killings, he and his clan members decided to take retribution against the other clan. They discovered where the murderers had fled and surrounded the camp; her father ordered his men, "'Point your guns and arrows at all those men and don't miss any. Kill them all at once.' . . . The seven men who came out of the wickiup were shot down and killed right there." Two years later, the offending clan made contact with Anna Price's clan, offering to make a settlement. After a great deal of talking, Anna's father finally said, "Very well, it will be all right that way."[17] The offending clan members were allowed to return to their homes as the feud had been resolved.

Any homicide that occurred within the tribe could be resolved by giving satisfaction to the aggrieved party. Morris Edward Opler explains that "they may insist upon his surrender and death, even though refusal of their demands leads frequently to armed conflicts and a feud between the families." This custom suggests that a killing could be paid back and both sides would then be even. However, if a killing had occurred and "the killer is not given up by his family, usually a fight between the families takes place." If an intermediary could arrange a settlement it might prevent a feud that could continue for decades. The negotiator would try to arrange for the killer and his family to make a payment of horses, guns, or other items of value to the family of the victim or to his friends. "Sometimes relatives of the slain person may be satisfied with physical punishment of the murderer."[18]

If the killer had been a constant troublemaker, his family may have been unwilling to defend him and would instead give him up. Or the killer may take flight, leaving the area, and remaining away until the bitterness against him and his crime subsided. When killings occurred, the family of the aggressor had the duty to solve the dispute between the two families. The leader of the clan would try to arrange for compensation to right the wrong committed by his band member, but the hostility often smoldered for years and could flare up again, resulting in a rival killing as payback. This scenario helps to explain killings that occurred many years later during or after tiswin parties; the aggrieved party often carried a grudge that resurfaced while drinking.

Whenever an accidental killing occurred, the aggrieved party often attempted to get even. To prevent this, the killer had to pay compensation, especially if demanded by a brother or other close relative. Such payments would usually be horses, blankets, buckskin, or similar valuable items. Refusal to pay often caused a dangerous feud between the two families. After accidental deaths the killer's family would send the best talkers to negotiate with the aggrieved party. Because of familial relationship, "the mother of the man in trouble might play a prominent part in such negotiations." Chiefs and other prominent members of the clan might also become involved in the discussions between the two families. The family of the killer had to offer an agreed-upon payment to the aggrieved party. "The payment was either burned on the spot or taken home and used. If the horses which were given as part of the payment were killed, their meat was eaten."[19]

Goodwin discovered that interband killings often happened when men were gambling or quarreling over women. "Most of the killings recorded seem to have occurred during or following drinking parties, when slightly intoxicated men were likely to become argumentative, recall old grudges, and pick a fight."[20] Sometimes, when the killing was inexcusable, the family of the murderer might abandon him, fail to protect him, and give "him up to the family of the murdered person, meaning that this family could kill on sight."[21] By doing this, they eliminated the danger of being attacked by the aggrieved family.

Although their belief systems were quite different from those of white society, the Apaches possessed deep-rooted moral values that paralleled the white social code. Frank C. Lockwood observes that the Apache "adhered more strictly to his social code than the white man does to his."[22] Apache society provided various rules to control social and criminal behavior; however, their lifestyle posed insurmountable problems, and Arizona territorial officials refused to tolerate blood feuds and retaliation killings as a form of social behavior.[23]

CASADORA–CAPTAIN JACK RIVALRY

During the nineteenth century, the federal government tried to identify Apache band members by assigning numbers to each married man and requiring that he wear a small metal tag inscribed with a number around his neck. Because Apache names were difficult to pronounce and spell, white authorities believed this system to be the solution for the problem of identifying the men. Goodwin notes that "each tag band had a chief selected and recognized by the government, who always was given the number 1."[24] Casadora was assigned number SJ-1, and Captain Jack received SC-1. Normally, after a tag band chief died or was killed, another man was selected by the band members to take his place. However, his widow received the band tag number 1. The use of tags for identification continued into the twentieth century, but was slowly phased out. As late as 1912, the San Carlos census still assigned tag band numbers to all married Indian men. Goodwin encountered examples of it as late as the 1930s while completing his research on Apache social organization.[25]

As already suggested, there were feuds among Apache bands in Arizona Territory during the nineteenth century. The problem may have been aggravated by congregating many different bands together at San Carlos. Bands that may have lived many miles from each other before were now living near bands with whom they may have experienced deadly disputes in the past. This helps to explain what happened in early

1888, a few miles north of the San Carlos Agency. Exactly when or how the feud between Captain Jack's SC band and Casadora's SJ band originated is unknown; however, some information suggests that Casadora had a history of difficulty with other bands as well.

Indian agent John P. Clum relates that Cochise advised him that Casadora, chief of the Coyotero Apaches, was on friendly terms with the whites around San Carlos and would cooperate with him to protect American citizens "from bad Apaches."[26] In 1873, several Chiricahua engaged in a tiswin party and then killed two Americans. Fearing retribution from the U.S. Army, many of the Apache bands quickly left the San Carlos Agency. Although Casadora also fled, Clum suggests that "no man, white or red, was more tractable or more peacefully inclined than Casadora." The Indian agent naively suggests that Casadora "had never even been accused of wrong-doing."[27] During this dispute, Casadora sent a woman to make contact with Captain Hamilton, who was in command of forces seeking to capture or destroy these "renegades," to tell him that they wanted to surrender and return to San Carlos. Captain Hamilton refused. The next morning, Hamilton's sentries informed the captain that a large group of Apache "men, women, and children, with hands upraised" were approaching the camp. After some preliminary discussion, Captain Hamilton agreed to talk with the Apaches. When he reached the picket line, he found "Casadora and his entire band" wanting to surrender. Casadora claimed that he had been forced to leave the agency for fear of retribution for the killing of two white men by the Chiricahua. He pleaded, "We cannot fight. We have no guns, no bullets. We have no food."[28] After examining Casadora's band, Captain Hamilton agreed not to attack them. Within a few days, all of the Apaches returned to San Carlos. Three years later, John Clum arranged to take an Apache delegation that included Diablo, Eskiminizin, Captain Jim of the agency police, Casadora, Tahzay, Captain Chiquito, and their wives to Washington, D.C.[29] In Clum's version, Casadora could do no wrong.

There was, however, another side to Casadora that reflects a tendency toward violence against other Apaches. David Longstreet, while serving as a sergeant of Apache scouts, claimed that Casadora "had killed one woman and shot one man in the nose." Because of these assaults, Casadora "took his people out on the warpath in the hills." According to Longstreet, Casadora had been living near Peridot at the time, suggesting that the event probably occurred in the 1880s. Casadora, although fearing a deadly feud, chose not to negotiate with the victim's clan and instead "led his people up the San Carlos River some ten miles above Rice." He and his band took up a position on Black Mesa, probably a few miles south of the Casadora Mountains, where they built fortifications to defend themselves. Keith H. Basso claims that "once branded a murderer, he [Casadora] had no choice but to turn 'renegade' and face the consequences of having broken reservation law."[30] Longstreet recalled that Casadora's band shot at him and the other scouts sent out to bring them in. Longstreet notes that "one of the scouts got shot through the chest and the bullet came out his back." Despite talking with them, Casadora refused to surrender. After sending word to San Carlos, the army sent out a detachment of soldiers with more scouts.[31] John Rope, another Apache scout, said that when he arrived at Black Mesa, he attempted to arrest Casadora. Rope related that Casadora's band began to shoot at them, killing one scout and wounding another, and "that night we scouts were set at the place where the scout got killed."[32] Refusing to submit to arrest by the San Carlos scouts, Casadora and his band remained in their fortified position; however, they eventually surrendered five days later to white authorities in Globe, Arizona.[33]

Goodwin's interviews with Rope and Longstreet revealed that in late 1887 members of Casadora's band had killed at least two of Captain Jack's band members somewhere along the San Carlos River. The victims were believed to have been Captain Jack's father and a brother.[34] Several months later, in early 1888, Casadora's men killed another man. Rope described what happened: "One man who had joined the scouts . . . was a good fellow and not married. He was riding along by Peridot one day and some Indians killed him."[35] The victim was an Apache scout and a member of Captain Jack's band. San Carlos scouts arrested the two men accused in the killing and placed them in the guardhouse; however, one escaped. It is possible that Casadora's trip to Washington, D.C., in the late 1870s may have increased his influence at San Carlos, and he may have been able to get the charges dropped for the second suspect. There are no records of the arrest or prosecution of Casadora's men. This increased the anger and resentment held by Captain Jack and, of course, he wanted retribution.[36] As late as the 1870s, the federal government accepted Indian control and punishment of criminal offenses on the reservations. The 1874 revised statute stated that although all federal laws "shall extend to the Indian country," they do not apply "to any Indian committing any offense in the Indian country who has been punished by the local law of the tribe."[37] Apparently, the death of this scout sparked the reprisal killing by Captain Jack's band. The original cause of the feud, however, remains unclear. Feuds, of course, were serious business and, as discussed earlier, the band members of the attackers had to resolve the dispute quickly with the victim's band or face retribution that could be deadly. There is no indication that Casadora or any of his band members attempted to reach a settlement with Captain Jack for any of these killings. According to Apache tribal custom, if the aggrieved party did not receive an acceptable payment from the family or clan member who committed the killing, Captain Jack had to take retribution; otherwise he and his band members would lose face in the Apache community.

GILA COUNTY CRIMINAL JUSTICE SYSTEM

The Gila County criminal justice system operated under the rules established by the U.S. Congress and the territorial legislature. To address crime during the territorial period, it employed a joint-control system with powers shared within federal and county jurisdictions. Originally, the federal district courts possessed jurisdiction over criminal cases that occurred on federal military posts and Indian reservations. Federal law recognized only one form of murder, first degree. Federal statute title 70, chapter 3, section 5339 states, "Every person who commits murder . . . within any fort . . . or in any other place or district of county under the exclusive jurisdiction of the United States . . . shall suffer death."[38] Cases prosecuted under this statute usually occurred on government military posts or on board U.S. war vessels or merchant ships. Territorial law, however, differentiated between first- and second-degree murder; only defendants charged under the former were placed at risk to pay the supreme penalty. The passage of the Indian Appropriation Act of March 3, 1885, commonly called the Major Crimes Act, modified the territorial legal system by placing seven serious crimes (including homicide) under the jurisdiction of the local territorial courts that convened in the various county seats, even if the crime was committed on an Indian reservation. In 1886, the U.S. Supreme Court decision *U.S. v. Kagama* held that Congress had a right to pass such legislation to control behavior on Indian reservations, therefore the Major Crimes Act was legal and binding. This decision clarified the federal criminal jurisdiction under the new law.[39] The enforcement of federal and territorial criminal law in the West changed significantly with the development of Indian reservations during the second half of the nineteenth century. Even in 1887, however, legal jurisdiction over Apaches committing homicides in Arizona Territory was not entirely clear.

In the late nineteenth century, the Arizona territorial criminal justice system was controlled by whites, many of whom perceived Apaches as a threat. Apaches and other Indians who could neither vote nor serve on juries lived virtually unprotected in an "alien" legal world. In 1883, while discussing justice in America, Robert G. Ingersoll observed: "We must remember that we have to make judges out of men, and that by being made judges their prejudices are not diminished and their intelligence is not increased."[40] A little over a decade later, in an address delivered January 17, 1899, Oliver Wendell Holmes suggested that one of the "gravest defects [of juries is] . . . that they will introduce into their verdict a certain amount—a very large amount, so far as I have observed—of popular prejudice, and thus keep the administration of the law in accord with the wishes and feelings of the community."[41] These two views of judges and juries may help to explain what happened to Captain Jack and other Apache defendants in Arizona Territory.

The judge and the jury play two very different but important roles in a criminal trial. The judge interprets and applies the law, controls the procedures during the trial, and acts as a mediator between the two opposing sides—prosecution and defense. The jury's duty is to determine the facts, or more precisely, to decide which witnesses to believe and which ones to discount because they are either lying or unreliable. The jurors must adhere to the law as stipulated and explained by the judge, but they have the right to reach their own verdict based upon the facts.[42] The jury trial is not an exact science. In 1872, in *Roughing It*, Mark Twain mocked justice by suggesting that "the jury system puts a ban upon intelligence and honesty, and a premium upon ignorance, stupidity and perjury."[43] Twain's harsh assessment notwithstanding, it was and is hard to find twelve good and true jurors to evaluate the evidence in a fair manner under the supervision of a judge who ensures that justice prevails.

Forming the jury usually begins with the sheriff bringing in a roster with about fifty names of people (all men in 1888) who are of voting age and selected from the list of all eligible voters in the county. The sheriff's list is commonly called a venire, and the people on it are ordered to appear at the courthouse and to be ready to serve on a jury if they are chosen. Normally the sheriff brings in these prospective jurors for the voir dire examination. At this stage, both the prosecutor and the defense counsel are allowed to ask prospective jurors questions to determine if they know the defendant, to ascertain whether they have made up their minds about his guilt or innocence, to inquire whether they or family members previously have been victims of similar crimes, and to assess whether prejudice exists. During this process, both sides may reject prospective jurors, each, of course, trying to keep people off the jury who might diminish their chances of winning the case.

In the American legal system there has always been the illusion that the jury is a cross section of society or at least an impartial group.[44] However, such a jury did not exist for Indian, Chinese, black, or Hispanic defendants in Arizona Territory, or, for that matter, anywhere else in the United States at the end of the nineteenth century. Since the impaneling testimony of the jury is not available, we can only speculate on what the dynamics were like during the voir dire process. Juries in nineteenth-century Arizona Territory were composed almost exclusively of white males, with Hispanics serving on juries in certain counties. The same was true of the prospective jurors in Maricopa County. For Native Americans like Captain Jack, the old adage that a person has the right to be judged by a jury of his "peers" was an illusion in 1888.

During the nineteenth century, ethnic defendants were viewed as exceedingly different by the dominant society. For example, Captain Jack, an Apache, spoke a "foreign" language, lived a very different lifestyle from white settlers, and adhered to radically different cultural norms that probably seemed out of place to most members of Arizona Territory's white society. The dominant society perceived Chinese and Indians as social misfits. Ethnic defendants who appeared before all-white juries had higher conviction rates and received more severe punishment than white defendants charged with similar crimes.[45] White juries found it difficult to relate to or to even understand Indian defendants. It is very doubtful that any of the jury members understood Apache culture; it is also unlikely that they accepted the constitutional concept that Captain Jack was their equal before the law.

One of the unusual aspects of the jury trial system is that twelve disparate people, who probably do not know one another (unless they live in a very small community), are selected to serve for a short, unspecified length of time and then, after the trial, return to their homes to continue their normal routines. Unfortunately, in the case of *U.S. v. Captain Jack,* scant evidence exists regarding the jurors. We will never know whether these were "twelve angry men" who may have jumped to conclusions regarding an Indian's guilt, or whether they methodically evaluated the evidence against Captain Jack.

What we do know, however, is that Indian defendants charged with murder had little chance of being acquitted, especially if they were accused of killing white victims. Recent research has revealed that nineteenth-century Arizona Territory juries convicted 86 percent of Apache defendants charged with murder or manslaughter, while white defendants had a 38 percent rate.[46] It is clear that juries viewed Indian defendants and their crimes in a very different light than white defendants; the race of the victim and killer mattered to these juries.

THE TRIAL OF CAPTAIN JACK

As suggested already, Captain Jack entered the white-dominated criminal justice system in Arizona Territory at a great disadvantage and extreme risk. In addition to the all-white jury, judge, and attorneys and the court-appointed counsel, Captain Jack didn't understand the language of the court, and the court did not understand him. Two interpreters were required to translate to and from Apache, and testimony often became scrambled. His cultural background did not adequately prepare him to deal with court testimony and cross-examination. He did not know how the criminal justice system worked. In effect, he was thrust into a bewildering world that must have been a mystery to him.

Because Captain Jack was indigent, William W. Porter, U.S. court justice, appointed H. N. Alexander and L. H. Chalmers as defense counsel; they were selected from those attorneys that were present in the courtroom. Unfortunately for Captain Jack, his legal counsel normally practiced civil law and had little experience in criminal law, especially with felony charges of murder.[47] On May 15, 1888, L. H. Orme, foreman of the grand jury of the U.S. District Court, Second Judicial District, County of Maricopa, Arizona Territory, filed an indictment for

murder against Captain Jack, Tzayzintilth, Hastindutody,
Ilthkah, Lahcohn, and Tillychillay. They were charged with
killing Nachona on or about April 10, 1888, within the
Second Judicial District. On May 19, Alexander and
Chalmers, the court-appointed defense counsel, filed a
demurrer to the indictment against Captain Jack and his codefendants. They asserted "that this Court has no jurisdiction in
the above entitled case by reason of its not being within the
legal jurisdiction of said Court."[48] They claimed that the federal authorities had no authority to "hear and determine this
case, nor jurisdiction of the person of the defendant." Defense
counsel argued that the defendant, an Apache, had been
charged with killing an Indian within the Second Judicial District, but the indictment named no county. Further, the indictment was ambiguous as to the specific locality and time of the
killing. Finally, the indictment alleged that the crime had been
"committed 'on or about the 10th day of April 1888.'" The
defense claimed that this was too vague.[49] The next day, Judge
William W. Porter overruled the demurrer, the defendants pled
not guilty, and defense counsel moved for a separate trial for
Captain Jack, which was granted by the court. On May 21,
1888, Captain Jack was tried by the U.S. District Court in
Phoenix, Maricopa County, Arizona Territory. After the
reading of the indictment, J. M. Montoya and Antonio Díaz
were sworn in to act as interpreters.[50]

THE CRIME

Casadora and his band lived near the Lutheran Mission
approximately one mile north of Peridot. On April 10, 1888, he
and eight men were traveling south to the San Carlos Agency, a
distance of about seven or eight miles, apparently to replace the
band tags of two men who had lost theirs.

When visiting the agency, Casadora and his SJ tag band sometimes traveled along a road that passed by Captain Jack's camp, even though Casadora must have been acutely aware of the nature of the dispute he was having with the SC band chief. Captain Jack's camp was situated about one hundred yards from the road, where he and his men had developed a small *ranchería* of wickiups next to two houses owned by Nalgada (SD band chief) and Algoden. The camp was about three to four miles north of San Carlos. Even though there were other trails that took a different route to the agency, Casadora preferred to take this main road. Casadora was riding with eight men, six of them armed, and they were about to pass by Captain Jack's camp when the shootings occurred. Nachona and Nasua were leading the column of Casadora's band and, as they approached the camp, one or more of Captain Jack's band members spotted them and noticed that some were carrying rifles. John Rope, an Apache scout who later joined other scouts to arrest them, explained that when Casadora's men reached Captain Jack's camp, four men shot and killed Nachona and Nasua. Rope claimed that the two victims had been "relatives of the people that had killed the scout," a member of Captain Jack's band, two months earlier.[51] Apparently, Captain Jack and his men, after spotting Casadora's men, were about one hundred yards from the road; consequently, four men ran out about fifteen or twenty yards before they fired four shots, killing the two men who were riding in front of the group. Then they quickly fired four more shots at Casadora's band, which then raced down the road south over a hill to safety and continued on to the San Carlos Agency. Casadora, an influential chief and well known at San Carlos, immediately complained to Colonel Simon Snyder and demanded that he arrest Captain Jack and his men. These killings occurred just three years after the passage of the

Major Crimes Act of 1885, which had turned jurisdiction for homicide and other major crimes over to the federal government and, in some cases, local county authorities. Prior to this law, and under Apache tribal law, these two killings would be considered a "just" retribution by Captain Jack for the previous murders by Casadora's band. In the past these killings would have been resolved by negotiation between the two bands; however, in this case, Casadora received a sympathetic hearing from Colonel Snyder, who had orders to arrest all Apaches who violated the Major Crimes Act of 1885.

After some discussion between Colonel Snyder and Casadora, the colonel sent Captain P. L. Lee to arrest the accused. Captain Lee assigned John Rope and several other Apache scouts to accompany him. They traveled up the valley and quickly reached Captain Jack's camp. After some negotiating, Captain Jack and his men agreed to surrender if they were protected by the U.S. Army. Captain Lee returned to the agency and quickly received approval from Colonel Snyder to use wagons and a detachment of scouts to bring them in safely. Things became tense, however, when some of Casadora's band members threatened to shoot. John Rope claimed that "pretty soon four army wagons drove up" to safely bring the suspects back to San Carlos.[52] Captain Lee and the scouts carried Captain Jack's band members to the agency without incident and had them delivered to the San Carlos guardhouse to await legal action.

THE PROSECUTION'S CASE

Owen T. Rouse, the U.S. attorney, and his staff developed a strong case against Captain Jack. They had at least seven eyewitnesses to the alleged crime and two army officers, who had arrested and incarcerated Captain Jack and his band members.

San Carlos Guardhouse and Indian Police, 1880. Apache defendants were incarcerated here before their trials. *Courtesy Arizona State Library, Archives and Public Records, Phoenix, No. 95-2823*

The prosecutors also had obtained incriminating statements made by Captain Jack before the killings. One of the officers had talked with Captain Jack about his dispute with Casadora just one week before the killings. This conversation proved to be incriminating and provided a plausible and very strong motive of revenge for the killings. Unfortunately, Apaches did not know their legal rights and were unaware that any statements they made to arresting officers or to jailers could be used against them by the prosecution. Equally important, the defense counsel placed Captain Jack on the stand to testify, a risky move, which opened him up to damaging cross-examination that could strengthen the prosecution's case. Add to this an all-white, and probably unsympathetic, jury and you have a strong case for murder.

On May 21, 1888, U.S. Attorney Rouse began by calling Casadora to testify. When asked what happened while he was riding to the agency, Casadora pointed at Captain Jack and stated that Captain Jack and his five band members shot at him and killed two of his men, Nachona and Nasua. At the urging of the prosecution, the witness identified Hastindutody and Tillychillay as the ones who had shot Nachona. Rouse asked him to explain exactly how the killings occurred. Casadora testified that he and eight band members were riding horses south down the main road from Peridot toward the San Carlos Agency when they were about to pass by Captain Jack's camp near Nalgada's house.[53] The accused had been living next to two houses, one of which was owned by Nalgada, chief of the SD tag band and Algoden, another tag band leader. Casadora saw Captain Jack with a gun standing in front of Algoden's house, about one hundred yards from the road. It was about 11 a.m. and they were going to the agency to get new tags for Nasua and Nachona. He pointed at the six defendants and stated that they were standing up by the houses near the road—when he and his men approached the camp. Asked about how the shooting occurred, Casadora replied that there was no warning; Captain Jack's men did not say anything before they shot at him and his band with Winchester rifles. Nachona, the first victim, received wounds in the chest; however, Nasua was the "man that died first."[54] Casadora claimed that he saw both men being shot; there were four shots from the group and then four more. The witness testified that he and his men did not return fire; instead they quickly rode to safety and continued on to San Carlos.[55]

During cross-examination, defense counsel H. N. Alexander asked Casadora about his relationship with Captain Jack. The witness claimed that he lived "about four miles" north of Captain Jack's place and had known him for several years. When asked whether his men were carrying rifles to visit the agency, he admitted that six of his men, including Nachona and Nasua, who were leading the group down the road, were armed. Defense counsel asked the witness: "Didn't you know there was a rule against Indians carrying arms when going to the agency?" The prosecution objected and was sustained. Asked why they were carrying weapons, Casadora replied: "We carried our arms because we have always been in the habit of carrying arms there and would put them away before we got to the agency." Alexander inquired why they would hide their weapons before entering the agency, and the prosecution objected but was overruled. Casadora answered: "We were going to hide them because there was a rule no Indian should carry arms around the agency."[56] Finally, defense counsel demanded to know why he had taken six men who were armed. He replied that they were going to play some games at the agency and to "buy goods." Alexander asked again why they carried their arms, and he replied: "To kill rabbits, hares and squirrels."[57]

When the prosecutor called Ztalnaki to testify, he asked him what his Apache name meant in English. Ztalnaki replied: "Cunt of the prairie."[58] The witness testified that he, Casadora, Luchua, Gagol, Guda, Taguchua, Dastha, Nasua, and Nachona were riding south toward the agency and were about to pass Nalgada's house when they were confronted by Captain Jack, Hastindutody, Ilthkah, Tzayzintilth, Lahcohn, and Tillychillay. Ztalnaki claimed that when Casadora and his band approached Captain Jack's place, Nasua, who was riding in front, asked them, "What are you going to do?" Almost immediately one of them answered him, "This," and shot at Casadora's tag band, killing Nasua and Nachona.[59] The witness testified that all of Captain Jack's band members shot at once after the first shot. Ztalnaki also claimed that Captain Jack and another man were in a hole that had been dug beside the house. During cross-examination, the witness admitted that Nasua and Nachona were armed with rifles. He testified that none of Casadora's band, however, shot back at Captain Jack's band and, after the shooting, "we ran up a hill from the road and came right down to the agency."[60]

U.S. Attorney Rouse called Gagol to testify and asked him who was shot first. Gagol responded: "The first bullet killed a man—Nasua, and immediately after that one other Nachona." During cross-examination by Alexander, Gagol was asked about the holes that were along the road, where some of Captain Jack's men were allegedly hiding before shooting. He claimed that anyone hiding in the holes could not be seen. He also admitted that he did not see anyone in the holes during the shooting. Gagol: "When we were shot at, I did not see the holes, the only time I saw the holes was when I came back with the officers." Asked if they fired at him from the holes, he said: "No sir, not from the holes but near the road."[61] Alexander asked, "Is it possible for a person coming from the ranch of Casadora to get to the agency without passing Capt. Jack's house along that road?" Gagol replied, "There are trails going from the ranch to the agency, but we are in the custom of going by this main road."[62]

The prosecutor called Captain P. L. Lee, an army officer assigned to duty at San Carlos, to testify. He stated that around 10 a.m. on April 10, Colonel Simon Snyder had been informed that "some Indians had been killed a few miles from the post." Captain Lee was given orders to take a detachment of about six or seven Apache scouts, locate the crime scene, and arrest those responsible for the killings. When he arrived within a mile of Captain Jack's camp, Captain Lee "met a squaw who informed [him] they had intrenched [sic] themselves, were drunk and going to fight. I got a little closer half a mile, when Captain Jack's mother came up and I told her to go and tell him I wanted him to give himself up." Later she returned and said that Captain Jack "would like to speak with me, he came out perhaps fifty yards from the building, and stated that he had no quarrel with the whites."[63] After talking for a while, Captain Jack "finally agreed if I would protect him he would give himself up." Lee found a "body lying in the road" and, about fifty yards farther, a second body also lying near the road. Although the second victim was still alive, he died within about fifteen minutes. Lee testified that he arrested "Captain Jack, and five others, I cannot recall their names, I don't know Indian."[64] Lee noticed that the band members had recently dug several pits in the ground and had guns and ammunition lying by them. The two bodies were around seventy-five yards from the building that was set back from the road. Lee claimed that the killings occurred "about three miles" northwest of the agency. During cross-examination, Alexander asked, "Now in regard to these rifle pits, were they newly dug?" Lee replied, "Yes sir." The captain believed that they had been scooped out by Captain Jack's men to ward off a possible attack by Casadora's band members, some of whom were armed, if they had returned to the crime scene.[65] Lee testified that the region around the shooting site was rough country. He admitted that he had used an interpreter to converse with Captain Jack; Lee spoke neither Apache dialects nor Spanish.

U.S. Attorney Rouse called Colonel Simon Snyder. He testified that he had received information that some of Captain Jack's band had killed some of Casadora's men. He ordered Captain Lee to "proceed to the scene and stop any further fighting and arrest all concerned in the killing and bring them to the post." Lee returned quickly to the agency and advised Snyder that Captain Jack agreed to surrender and "asked that I would send some wagons to bring their effects and all their families into the post."[66] Snyder sent the wagons to pick them up and had them all at the San Carlos Agency before dark.

Snyder admitted that he did not see or know exactly which Indians had come in. After inspecting the guardhouse report, however, he noticed Captain Jack's name on the list. During cross-examination, defense counsel asked Snyder how long he had been in command at San Carlos. He stated that he arrived there on March 19, 1888, and took command three days later. Alexander: "Have you studied the manners and customs of these Indians to any extent?" Snyder replied, "No sir, I never have to any extent, I never had any experience prior to my arrival at San Carlos."[67] In other words, Colonel Snyder had been on duty for about twenty days and certainly did not have any firsthand knowledge about Apaches and their social manners. Alexander inquired, "Was the conversation that you related here that you had with Captain Jack before the killing through the aid of an interpreter?" Snyder answered, "Yes sir, through the official interpreter."[68] Alexander asked him whether he had become aware from his conversation with Captain Jack that the Apaches had "customs of avenging themselves." Prosecutor Rouse objected and was sustained. Unable to pursue this tactic, Alexander had no further questions. Turning to the judge, U.S. Attorney Rouse said, "We rest."

The prosecution had presented a strong case against the defendant. They had placed him and his men at the scene of the crime by using the testimony of Casadora and two of his band members. These eyewitnesses testified that Captain Jack and five band members had fired at least eight shots, killing Nasua and Nachona. All three witnesses provided significant details revealing where the killers were standing, the distance from the defendants' camp to the road, what kinds of weapons they used, and the number of shots taken by Captain Jack's band members. The evidence was very strong and was buttressed by the testimony of Captain P. L. Lee and Colonel Simon Snyder, who listened to Casadora's complaint and then effected the arrest of the suspects. Defense counsel would have a difficult task trying to refute this testimony or sway the jury to agree that their client was not guilty of murder.

THE DEFENSE'S CASE

Defense counsel H. N. Alexander began his defense by calling Captain Jack to testify. This legal maneuver is risky because it opens up the defendant to cross-examination by the prosecution, and if he has anything to hide, it could be exposed during this cross-examination. Alexander began his questioning by asking Captain Jack to "tell the jury all about" the shootings that occurred on April 10, 1888. Captain Jack began: "I was at my home working there that morning" when he saw Casadora's men "coming down towards my place." The witness noticed that some of Casadora's band members were carrying guns. He said, "There was a rule that no Indian should come armed to the Agency." Because they approached armed with rifles, Captain Jack believed that he and his men "were going to be attacked, and we prepared ourselves and as they came close, we fired and killed one Indian there and after they ran away one shot was fired back from Casadora's band and then our band fired four shots."[69] When asked how many band members were involved in the shooting, he answered four, "Hastindutody, Tzayzintilth, Lahcohn, and Ilthkah." He stated that only these four men actually shot at Casadora's band; he also had a gun, but "I did not shoot." Neither did Tillychillay; Captain Jack said that "he was down on the river among the cottonwoods doing a job there and heard the shooting." Captain Jack admitted that they dug pits right after the shooting "because we were afraid Casadora and his band would come and jump us." He did not order his men to dig the pits; "My men made them because they were afraid of this other band." Alexander asked how far the pits were from the road. He replied, "About 100 yards." Asked if the holes were dug "after or before the shooting?" Captain Jack answered, "After."[70]

As suggested earlier, this shooting incident had a history that extended back six months to a year, and possibly more; the court testimony and the San Carlos records make it clear that this blood feud between the SC and SJ tag bands had been deadly. During cross-examination, defense counsel Alexander, addressing this dispute between the two bands, asked Casadora if there were "any ill feeling between your band and Capt. Jack's before the shooting?" Casadora admitted that about a month before, an "Indian . . . belonging to Capt. Jack's band, he was killed by some of my men."[71]

Defense counsel also asked Captain Jack about the dispute when he took the stand. Alexander: "Was there any ill feeling between Captain Jack and his band and Casadora and his band before this day of the shooting?" Captain Jack answered, "Yes sir, they were mad at each other . . . because Casadora's Indians had killed one of our men." Asked about others who might be involved in the dispute, Captain Jack claimed that Tillychillay had not been living with his band until just recently. Captain Jack explained that Casadora's band had killed a scout and since Tillychillay was related to the scout, he "was afraid he would be killed and came down" for protection.[72] During cross-examination, Rouse asked about the relationship between the two bands prior to the earlier shooting. Captain Jack replied, "Before the killing of my man we liked each other well, we used to eat at the same table, were great friends, but since the killing of my man, we got mad at each other." Asked if he "hated Casadora and his band," Captain Jack replied, "I will ask you if you had a brother killed would you not hate the killer? I so hate them since they killed that man." The witness also admitted that he had explained to Colonel Snyder that "I was feeling bad, could not eat or sleep thinking about their killing my man."[73] Asked how long before the shooting one of his band had been killed by Casadora, he replied: "One hundred and sixty-six days ago from the time of the killing to this day."[74] There is some disagreement about the date of the killing of the scout; the other band members testified that the killing of the scout was about one or two months previous. Captain Jack may have been referring to earlier killings.

During his testimony for the prosecution, Snyder stated that "he told me that some men belonging to another band or bands had killed three of his people, among them his father, I think I understood two were relatives of his, that he had never got satisfaction" for these killings. These murders had occurred about six months before the shooting of the scout. In his testimony, Snyder claimed that Captain Jack had said "it was customary among his people that where an Indian had killed in order to avenge him, that relatives of the Indian were justified in killing one of the other band in satisfaction." Captain Jack said that since no one had taken retribution against the other band, "it made him feel very bad, he could not eat, he could not sleep thinking about this all the time and he thought that the time had come for him to take action in the matter and he was going to settle it to suit himself."[75] When Captain Jack made these threats against Casadora, Colonel Snyder warned him that "he must not do anything of the kind . . . and if he did it, that I would see he was arrested and brought into prison."[76] Colonel Snyder claimed that this excited Captain Jack, who stated several times that he would take action against the other band. The Apaches' unique social legal system calling for retributive killings was unacceptable to local government; consequently, this sort of testimony was very damaging to the defense and was also difficult to counter.

When the defense called Tillychillay to testify, he admitted that he did not belong to Captain Jack's band but was a member of Touclis's band. Asked how long he had been living with Captain Jack's band, he replied, "I came down when they killed one of Jack's men." Asked why he had moved, he replied, "I was afraid to live there with my chief, because the Indian of Captain Jack's band that was killed was a relation of mine." Defense counsel: "What were you afraid of?" Witness: "I was afraid of Casadora's band, it was not the first time they had killed a man, and I was afraid they would kill me too."[77] He testified that he was not at the shooting, but was down by the San Carlos River working. Tillychillay stated, "I didn't see them, but heard them shoot, first I heard four shots, and I came out of the cottonwoods and saw the Indians, and I heard four shots again." As he came up to the road he saw Casadora's band race south toward the agency. Tillychillay asked one of the band members, "What are you shooting at?" He replied, "We shot at the fellows that run away, see the fellow there, we killed him."[78] Asked whether he had a gun at the time of the shooting, he replied, "My gun was in my tepee and I was down at the river without a gun." Asked whether he had been armed, the witness replied, "After the shooting I went to my tepee, took out my gun, and leaned it against my tepee." During cross-examination, prosecutor Rouse asked, "Did you ever hear Captain Jack make any threats against Casadora and his band and say what he was going to do?" Tillychillay replied, "No sir."[79]

After calling Hastindutody for the defense, Alexander asked him to "tell the jury all that happened that day." Hastindutody replied, "One of our men was killed in our band, and the day of the trouble, we saw Casadora and his band coming down armed and we got a little scared and suspected they wanted to jump us knowing that there was a rule no Indians should bear arms to the agency." Asked to name all those who were involved in the shooting, he responded, "Myself, Tzayzintilth, Ilthkah, and Lahcohn." He stated that Captain Jack and Tillychillay were not involved in the shootings.[80] Asked why they had fired at Casadora's men, he replied, "If we had seen them coming down without arms, we would not have done it, but we saw them coming down armed, with guns." During cross-examination, U.S. Attorney Rouse asked him how long prior to the shooting had Captain Jack's band member been killed. He replied, "About two months." Asked if he and "Captain Jack go down to the post with guns," he answered, "No, we did not take any arms because there was a rule any one going with arms would be put in the guard house."[81]

Defense counsel called Ilthkah and asked who had told him about Casadora's band killing a member of Captain Jack's band about two months before the shooting. He replied, "The evening that man was killed a man run down to us and told us, but when a man is killed at San Carlos every body knows it in a short time."[82] Alexander asked him about the shooting and why it had happened. Ilthkah replied, "Seeing that the brother of the Indian that had killed Captain Jack's Indian came there, we fired towards him; he fell and was killed." During cross-examination, assistant prosecutor A. C. Baker asked where the witness had been standing when the shooting began. Ilthkah replied that he and the other three shooters had run about "thirty steps from the house" toward the road before they shot. Asked whether Captain Jack had fired, he replied, "No he didn't, he had a gun in his hand but he didn't shoot, only four men shot."[83] Ilthkah also testified, "We did not dig the holes. The women dug the holes." They had been dug after the shooting because they feared an attack by Casadora's band. Asked whether Casadora had passed their camp before, Ilthkah answered, "I had seen them pass there several times, very often without any guns, this day they had some guns."[84]

Tzayzintilth, another defense witness, claimed that when they saw Casadora's band armed with rifles approaching, he, "Hastindutody, Ilthkah, and Lahcohn" all "fired at the brother of the Indian that killed one of Jack's Indians."[85] Lahcohn, another defense witness, claimed that they were in their wickiups and when they saw Casadora and his band approaching, they "were a hundred yards" away. He stated that when Casadora had passed the camp before two or three times they were "without guns."[86]

Finally, Alexander called Lieutenant Watson, 10th Cavalry, to testify as a character witness. He was asked how long he had known Captain Jack. Watson replied, "About two years and a half." After an inquiry about Captain Jack's demeanor, Watson answered, "He has the reputation of being a good man." Alexander asked, "What is said among the Indians as to his being a peaceable and quiet man?" Watson: "He has the reputation of being a peaceable, quiet man, friendly with the whites, well liked by them, and of not having any rows with other Indians."[87] During cross-examination, U.S. Attorney Rouse asked about Watson's duties at San Carlos. Watson replied, "I have been in charge of part of the Indians on the San Carlos Reservation." He admitted that he saw Captain Jack regularly, "nearly every day," during his tour of duty at San Carlos. Asked to name some of the whites at San Carlos who believed that Captain Jack was a peaceable man, Watson replied, "Captain Pierce, Benton formerly at San Carlos and there may be others, I remember those two names, I will say also that every one was much surprised he had been brought down."[88] This testimony, of course, supports the theory that Captain Jack had been very peaceful, at least before the killing of his band members.

Alexander, for the defense, closed his testimony and then presented two motions to the court. First, "that all the testimony of Captain Lee pertaining to the conversation that he had with Captain Jack . . . be stricken out on the grounds that it is hearsay evidence, that Jack never told him so, that it was what the interpreter said, that Jack told him so."[89] Baker, for the prosecution, countered: "The Defendant went on the stand and corroborated it and showed that he made it at that time. The point is this, the testimony as to this statement says that it was reached through an interpreter and it was confirmed by Captain Jack."[90] In rebuttal, Alexander responded: "At the time Captain Lee was giving that testimony I made a motion to strike it out, and I now move to strike out that portion of the testimony from the answer." Moving to his second motion, defense counsel Alexander: "I move to strike out all of the testimony of Colonel Snyder relative to the conversation that he had two or three days before this shooting with Captain Jack in his tent on the grounds that it is hearsay evidence and through an interpreter."[91] At that point the court reporter read the testimony of Captain Lee and the objection made at that time by Alexander for the defense. The next day, Tuesday, May 22, at 9 a.m., the court reconvened and the judge made a ruling: "I will now exclude from the testimony of Colonel Snyder and Captain Lee the conversation they had with Captain Jack, if you want to examine the witness again you can do it."[92] The prosecution and the defense closed their case and called for special instructions to the jury, which were resolved by the judge. The case was argued to the jury, and the court charged them and they retired to deliberate the case. Later that day, Charles A. Boake, foreman for the jury, delivered the verdict to the court. "We, the jury . . . find the defendant Captain Jack guilty of murder as charged in the indictment with recommendation to the mercy of the court."[93]

On June 5, 1888, defense counsel H. N. Alexander and L. H. Chalmers filed an arrest of judgment in open court. They argued "that the grand jury which found the indictment had no legal authority to inquire into the offense charged" because the crime had not been committed in Maricopa County and therefore was not under the jurisdiction of the U.S. District Court. Further, they argued "that the indictment is vague and uncertain as to time and locality."[94] Judge Porter overruled the defense's charges. On June 14, 1888, Judge William W. Porter sentenced Captain Jack to thirty years in the Ohio State Penitentiary, in Columbus.

TRIAL ANALYSIS

During this trial, the prosecution had a decided advantage over defense counsel for a variety of reasons. Captain Jack, by being indigent and an Apache, provided an easy case for U.S. Attorney Rouse to prosecute. White settlers in Arizona Territory had developed a deeply ingrained fear and hatred of Apaches. Geronimo, considered to be one of the worst enemies by many whites, had surrendered just two years earlier, and he and his Chiricahua band members had been sent off to prison at Fort Marion, Florida. The images of "ruthless" Apaches like Geronimo only intensified this hatred toward all Apaches. The fact that Captain Jack wanted revenge, and because he apparently refused to accept the Arizona territorial legal system, provided the prosecutor with motive for the killings and almost assured that he would gain a conviction.

This murder trial, which could have ended with a death sentence, lasted only one day and a few hours. This was a short murder trial even for the nineteenth-century American West. For example, Lawrence M. Friedman, in his discussion of crime and law in Alameda County, California, discovered that murder trials lasted "on the average, more than 7 full court days."[95] In Alameda County, of course, most of the defendants were white and, unless indigent, could afford competent legal defense. Captain Jack's abbreviated trial can be explained by a variety of factors. Captain Jack received a court-appointed attorney trained in civil law, which put the defendant in a very precarious position. Such legal representation proved to be inadequate for most Native Americans prosecuted for murder in Arizona Territory, California, and other regions of the American West as well. The court-appointed attorneys in Globe, Arizona, where most of these trials took place, usually received a fee of fifty dollars to defend their client. Any investigation of the facts about the crime or searching for character witnesses had to be paid out of pocket, while U.S. Attorney Rouse had the power of the U.S. government behind his prosecution of the defendant. Defense counsel H. N. Alexander and L. H. Chalmers, unfortunately, failed to develop any significant strategy to attack the credibility of the prosecution's witnesses. For example, there were several apparent inconsistencies in the testimony of Casadora, Gagol, and Ztalnaki; however, defense counsel failed to exploit these opportunities to increase Captain Jack's chances at acquittal. They should have attacked the credibility of the prosecution's witnesses' testimony, especially the claims by Casadora and Ztalnaki that Captain Jack fired at them. These claims were in direct conflict with the other witnesses, Hastindutody and Ilthkah. Why should the jury believe that the prosecution's testimony was any more reliable than the defense's witness? At least there was the possibility that defense counsel could have suggested that there certainly was a reasonable doubt. Testimony about the distance between Casadora and the shooters also called into question the veracity of the prosecution's witnesses. The distance between Captain Jack's camp and the road, as well as the position of Casadora's men are other issues that defense counsel could have used to attack the prosecution's witnesses. Equally important, defense counsel presented only one character witness, Lieutenant Watson, and his testimony indicated that there were other white military officers and possibly San Carlos support staff who could have testified to the character of the defendant, which might have swayed the jury. Even more important, defense counsel seemed more interested in filing an appeal with the U.S. Supreme Court than defending their client.

Finally, in any trial, especially a murder case, legal counsel's first and foremost duty is to develop the best defense possible.

They failed miserably in their attempt to meet that challenge. In their defense, the court appointed them less than a week before the trial began, which left them very little time to interview the defendants and prospective witnesses, and to arrange for them to come to court.

The use of two interpreters for the trial proved to be an important factor as well. J. M. Montoya and Antonio Díaz were sworn in to translate from Apache to Spanish to English and back again. There are inconsistencies in translation by the two interpreters that suggest that some of the testimony was being filtered and changed by Montoya and Díaz. For example, the use of the word *Indian* by Casadora, Captain Jack, and other Apache witnesses that appears in the transcript indicate the translation of the testimony was incorrect. *Indian* is a white man's construct that was alien to the Apaches. They might have used Coyotero, Pinal, San Carlos, Aravaipa, or another band affiliation, but not Indian. Finally, when defense counsel Alexander tried to pursue a discussion of the feud between Casadora and Captain Jack, Rouse objected and was sustained. Alexander should have been more forceful because this was the focus and the main reason for these killings. Defense counsel did not have to justify such Apache vendetta killings, but it might have helped to plant a reasonable doubt in the minds of one or more of the jurors.

EX PARTE CAPTAIN JACK

On July 23, 1888, U.S. Marshal W. K. Meade delivered Captain Jack, Hastindutody (twenty-five year sentence), Tillychillay (eighteen years), Lahcohn (fifteen years), Tzayzintilth (ten years), and Ilthkah (ten years) to the Ohio State Penitentiary in Columbus to serve out their sentences. He also delivered three other prisoners, Hahskingaygahlah, Miguel, and Sayes, and returned the certified copy of his report to the court on August 9, 1888.[96] After arriving at the Ohio State Penitentiary, the prison officials assigned inmate numbers and provided the age and height measurement for each Apache prisoner. Captain Jack was listed as thirty and five-feet-six-inches, and the jailer noticed a "bullet wound in right and left shoulders, bullet wound in right buttock." Tillychillay, listed as thirty-five and five-feet-six-inches, had a "bullet wound up out edge of right hand, up through forearm out at point of elbow, and two bullet wounds above right buttock, and one above right knee, and one on right front of shoulder." Lahcohn was twenty-eight and five-feet-eleven-inches tall. "Hastindutoday" was fifty-eight and five-feet-five-inches. Tzayzintilth, age nineteen, five-feet-six, had a tattoo on his forehead (arrow pointing up between two hills, with a line across the top and bottom) and on his left wrist and forearm. The jailer must have had a sense of humor: he listed habits of the inmates as "unknown, unless it be killing, scalping, etc." Hahskingaygahlah, age thirty-one, died February 9, 1889, and his body was delivered to the medical college February 10, 1889. Exactly one month later, Ilthkah, age twenty-one, died on March 9, 1889, and was buried at the prison on March 11, 1889.[97]

William H. Lamar, J. G. Zachry, and Samuel F. Phillips were retained as defense counsel, and they filed petitions for writs of habeas corpus for both Captain Jack and Gonshayee with the U.S. Supreme Court. Counsel argued that Captain Jack "is unlawfully and illegally detained and imprisoned by the warden, superintendent, or persons in charge in the State of Ohio, at the City of Columbus, in the State prison" as a federal prisoner. They noted that Captain Jack had been arrested, indicted, and convicted of murder by the U.S. District Court within the jurisdiction of the Second Judicial District of the Territory of Arizona. The defendant had been charged under the provisions of the Major Crimes Act of 1885.[98] Under this law, all Indians who commit murder, manslaughter, robbery, and four other major crimes "shall be tried therefor in the same courts . . . as are all other persons charged" with committing such crimes.[99] They argued that the crime was committed in Gila County and tried in Maricopa County under the jurisdiction of the U.S. statutes. Since the "U.S. Marshal summoned the grand and trial jurors, and not the sheriff of Gila County; that your petitioner is sentenced to imprisonment at a place without the Territory, all of which is contrary to the provisions of the penal code of Arizona. . . . That the said court had no jurisdiction to hear and determine this case."[100] Because the federal government did not have jurisdiction, they requested that a writ of habeas corpus be granted to Captain Jack, the petitioner.[101] On April 15, 1889, Justice Miller wrote the opinion for the U.S. Supreme Court, ruling that the petitioner had been tried within the wrong legal jurisdiction and that "writ of *habeas corpus* should issue."[102] This writ was served on the warden of the Ohio State Penitentiary, the prisoners were released by order of the U.S. Supreme Court on May 18, 1889, and they were transported by U.S. marshals back to San Carlos.

FINAL OBSERVATIONS

The reversal of the conviction, because it had been obtained by actions within the wrong jurisdiction, did not ensure that Captain Jack's ordeal had ended. Several months after being returned to San Carlos, the Gila County district attorney J. D. McCabe filed formal indictments for murder against Captain Jack, Tzayzintilth, Hastindutody, Lahcohn, and Tillychillay in the District Court, Second Judicial District, Territory of Arizona, Globe, Arizona Territory. All of them were charged with the killing of Nasua on April 10, 1888.[103] Judge Joseph H.

Kibbey presided over the trial, J. D. McCabe served as prosecutor, and E. H. Cook and H. V. Jackson represented the defendants. Unfortunately, there are no trial transcript notes for this second trial. Why the jury found Captain Jack not guilty is unknown. It is possible that he had better legal representation or, more likely, they believed the testimony that he did not fire his gun. From a cultural perspective it seemed logical that his band members committed the killing, not Captain Jack; it was their duty to take retribution. The jury, however, convicted all four of his band members and sentenced Tzayzintilth and Hastindutody to life in prison while Lahcohn and Tillychillay received ten years, each to be served in the Yuma Territorial Prison.[104]

In retrospect, the legal methods employed by the Arizona territorial criminal justice system had created a very serious dilemma for Captain Jack and his codefendants. For years they had lived by the social restrictions placed upon them by Apache tribal custom and law that required a settlement of a feud by peaceful means or else they must retaliate against the offending band. On the one hand, if Captain Jack failed to gain satisfaction, it was imperative that they kill a member of Casadora's band, otherwise he and his band members would lose face within the Apache community. On the other hand, if they killed in retribution, they would be tried, not by tribal law, but by Arizona territorial law.[105] It was a catch-22. This dramatic change of legal authority came quickly in the 1880s. In the late 1870s, Native Americans were still allowed to handle crime problems on reservations through tribal law; this was protected by federal statute.[106] In 1885, however, the U.S. Congress passed the Major Crimes Act. This law firmly established federal government control over crime in the American West, and the Arizona territorial criminal justice system governed Apache defendants accused of murder. These Apaches, as well as hundreds of other Native Americans, suffered under a legal system that saw them as outsiders who had to be controlled to protect the local white population. They were put at great risk, and many Apache defendants suffered the consequences—long periods of confinement in the Yuma Territorial Prison that could be deadly. Fortunately, the second jury saw fit to find Captain Jack not guilty. Considering how the criminal justice system treated Apaches, this, in itself, was remarkable.

CHAPTER 2

GONSHAYEE

The "Last Raid"

PURSUING THE HOSTILES

Lieut. Johnson's command surprised a murderous band of Apaches in the Rincon Mountains at noon Saturday capturing their baggage and horses. The Indians scattered among the rocks, and evidently will try to make their way back to San Carlos. . . . The troops are still in sharp pursuit.

New York Times, June 14, 1887

IN 1972, in *Ulzana's Raid,* film director Robert Aldrich used a remarkable historical event, completely rewrote the story, and turned it into a series of stereotypes that cast Apaches as ruthless villains. In the opening scene a group of soldiers are playing a ball game at Fort Lowell, Arizona, when a lone rider gallops in shouting, "Ulzana's gone out, Ulzana's gone out!"[1] The story begins with a discussion of Ulzana, a "renegade," leaving San Carlos Reservation to raid the surrounding countryside to "kill and maim" any unsuspecting whites living in the area.[2] In a film suffused with violence, Aldrich portrays Ulzana and his ten band members as "savages" of the worst sort. Graphic scenes include a dead farmer who has been tied to a stake with a fire set under his crotch area and a dog's tail stuffed in his mouth, a group of Apaches ruthlessly cutting out the heart of a young soldier with knives, and numerous other examples of the alleged Apache "savagery." In this film version, the cavalry eventually track down and kill Ulzana and all of his band.

Ironically, Ulzana, a Chiricahua Apache, did conduct a raid, but everything else in the film is pure fabrication. In November 1885, Ulzana crossed the border from Mexico into Arizona Territory, rode north, raided San Carlos Reservation for horses, killed several Apaches, captured some women, and lost one man, killed by a White Mountain Apache. Ulzana then headed south, fought and won a series of battles with the cavalry, killed thirty-eight victims, stole about 250 horses, changed mounts "at least twenty times," and eventually escaped back into Mexico with nine of his ten original band members.[3] This dramatic true story would have made a marvelous adventure film, but the director wanted the U.S. cavalry troopers to win; in the movies they always do.

Somewhat similar to the Ulzana story, although not as dramatic, the Gonshayee case contains elements that would make up what might be called the "last raid." In 1886, the removal of Geronimo and his Chiricahua band to Florida had apparently eliminated the last major resistance in the Southwest; it appeared that Apaches no longer threatened white settlers in Arizona Territory. Then suddenly, in June 1887, Gonshayee and members of his band, including Apache Kid, left San Carlos, split up into two groups, headed south, stole horses, and eventually killed two white settlers. Gonshayee, the band chief, acting as an intermediary with the U.S. Army, negotiated to allow Apache Kid, a first sergeant of Indian scouts, and four other scouts to return to San Carlos to submit to a court-martial for being away without leave and for attempted murder. Murder indictments were eventually brought against Gonshayee and several band members. This case study will examine and explain the origins and consequences of this "last raid" by Apaches in 1887.

THE POWER OF TISWIN

In the 1880s, Indian agents at San Carlos Reservation experienced significant difficulty trying to aid Apaches in adjusting to control by white authorities. By 1886, numerous Apache bands had been confined to the reservation without a substitute for their old lifestyle of raiding for cattle and horses. One can only imagine the difficulty that they must have experienced giving up the horse for farming in unproductive land along the Gila River. To escape the effects of disruptive culture shock that permeated San Carlos, Apaches turned more and more to drinking tiswin, an alcoholic beverage, as a way to relieve the oppressive drudgery of farming. Exactly when the Apaches first used tiswin is unclear; however, Morris Opler suggests that the beverage may have been inspired by Spanish-speaking people from the northern provinces of Mexico. Tiswin, made from corn, was a popular alcoholic drink at San Carlos. Although Apaches consumed mescal and other beverages, tiswin remained the favorite drink. The brewing process normally required several days to prepare tiswin, a beverage with about a 4 percent alcoholic content, and women who were proficient in making this drink were in high demand. The women would put ground corn into a pot and boil it until the water was reduced by half. Usually it took several hours to boil it down to the right mixture. Next they would fill the container to the top with water and boil it again until the mixture was a few inches from the top. Then the women would strain off the liquid, let it cool, and place it in large water jars. Normally it would be covered to allow the tiswin to ferment faster.[4] Women had their own ways of fixing tiswin from this point on. To give the drink a little kick, women

Apache woman making *tulapai,* 1880s. Tulapai, also called tiswin, was a popular beverage similar to beer. *Courtesy Arizona State Library, Archives and Public Records, Phoenix, No. 98-6082.*

sometimes added a short piece of jimsonweed root when they were boiling the brew. Later in the twentieth century, they used yeast to increase the fermentation process.[5] Captain John G. Bourke, an acute observer of Apache behavior at San Carlos, claimed that tiswin was "their sacred intoxicant." He also noted that tiswin was an important part of rituals for "Apache ceremonial dances."[6]

Before consuming tiswin, Apache males spent two to four days fasting because experience "taught them that it will more readily affect them through an empty stomach."[7] And, of course, under such conditions the alcoholic beverage had a dramatic effect on those who imbibed. These drinking episodes sometimes turned into wild melees frequently ending in death. White authorities had difficulty dealing with Apache customs, and tiswin drinking created many problems for the Indian agents and military officers trying to keep the peace. The various army officers who acted as Indian agents at San Carlos complained that the Apache men refused to be broken of the habit of drinking tiswin.[8] For example, in 1880, Indian Agent J. C. Tiffany reported that "the police force . . . have rendered efficient service in breaking up tis-win parties, and have destroyed no less than 2,000 gallons of the villainous drink." He noted that "there have been several Indians wounded in fights among themselves or at Tis-win parties; one man near [Fort] Apache killed; Chief Juh was stabbed by his squaw with a knife."[9] In 1889, Captain John L. Bullis complained, "The greatest drawback at the present time to the improvement of these people is the drinking of tis-win. . . . The result is generally a fight among themselves frequently ending in the killing of one or more."[10] Over a decade later another Indian agent reported, "The use of tiswin is much more difficult to prevent. . . . There has not been a time in their history when they can not remember having tiswin, and they claim it is both food and drink."[11]

General George Crook, commander of the U.S. Army in Arizona, tried numerous times to suppress the drinking of tiswin; he failed. During the 1880s, Lieutenant Britton Davis spent time with the Apaches and understood how some of them felt about white criticism of drinking tiswin. Davis recalled that General Crook had ordered all tiswin making at San Carlos to be stopped immediately. Davis called some of the chiefs in to talk to them about the tiswin problem, but he began by criticizing the Apache custom of wife beating. Nana, a well-known Chiricahua chief, did not like to be preached to by a young army officer. Just three years earlier Nana, in his eighties, with only a handful of men and women, left San Carlos and led a famous raid that frightened settlers and exhausted the U.S. Cavalry, which fought and lost a series of engagements. Davis insisted that his Apache scout Mickey Free translate exactly what Nana had said. Reluctantly, Free replied, "Tell the *Nantan Enchau* [stout chief] . . . that he can't advise me how to treat my women. He is only a boy. I killed *men* before he was born."[12]   Davis understood Nana's words and observed that when the Apaches had made peace with the Americans,

> nothing had been said about their conduct among themselves; they were not children to be taught how to live with their women and what they should eat or drink. All their lives they had eaten and drunk what seemed good to them. The white men drank wine and whiskey, even the officers and soldiers at the posts. The treatment of their wives was their own business. . . . Now they were being punished for things they had a right to do so long as they did no harm to others.[13]

The evidence is clear: tiswin proved to be a problem at San Carlos that would not go away, regardless of the attempts to suppress it, and the consequences of these drinking bouts could be far-reaching.

APACHE KID'S REVENGE

The origins of Apache Kid are sketchy; historian Dan Thrapp claims that Kid, the eldest son of Togodechuz, "had been born in Aravaipa Canyon," south of San Carlos. He was a member of the San Carlos SI band that had been led by his grandfather until his death, in December 1886. His real Apache name—there are at least eight possibilities—remains a mystery.[14] Kid married the daughter of Eskiminizin. The chief of the SL band, Eskiminizin lived in the Aravaipa Canyon near Captain Chiquito's SA band. Al Sieber, chief of scouts at San Carlos, took a liking to the boyish-looking young Apache and began to call

Apache Kid and codefendants at Globe, Arizona, 1889. Apache Kid is second from the right in the back row. *Courtesy of the Arizona Historical Society, Tucson, AHS No. 4542.*

him Kid. Sieber taught Kid some of the basics of being an army scout and encouraged him to enlist; he did so on August 1, 1883, listing his age as twenty-five, suggesting that he had been born in 1858. During this early period as an Apache scout, Kid saw service at the Big Dry Wash fight and was with General George Crook's command in Mexico in 1883. There are numerous stories about Kid's eyesight being "amazingly keen." It was reported that he could see things that many army officers could not even see with field glasses.[15] In 1885, Kid reenlisted for a second stint as a scout and returned to Mexico with Sieber's scouts in Crook's campaign against Geronimo and his

Chiricahua band. During a four-year period, Kid served as a scout under the commands of Captain Emmet Crawford, Lieutenant Britton Davis, and Lieutenant Dugan. He apparently showed great promise and quickly rose to the rank of first sergeant of Indian scouts in Company A.

In the 1850s, Togodechuz, Kid's father, and Rip, a member of Captain Chiquito's SA band, were competing for the hand of a beautiful Apache woman. After a period of courting and winning her hand, Togodechuz apparently gloated about it to his rival. Because of this, Rip developed a long-standing grudge against Togodechuz and Kid's grandfather as well. At Kid's court-martial, Captain F. E. Pierce testified that Kid's grandfather had been the leader of the SI band, and he had been killed in December 1886. Apparently, in December during a tiswin party, Rip goaded one of his drunken band members into stabbing and killing Kid's grandfather. After his death, the band members selected Gonshayee to serve as the new band chief. Whether the SI band members retaliated is unknown, but less than five months later, during another tiswin party in early May 1887, Rip encouraged Gonzizie, a fellow band member, to attack Togodechuz. Heavily under the influence of tiswin, Gonzizie shot and killed his victim.[16] Almost immediately, members of Gonshayee's SI band retaliated by killing Gonzizie. Kid, who was not present during the killing of his father, was not satisfied and wanted to gain revenge against Rip, the instigator of two SI band member killings. On May 28, 1887, Kid and four scouts left the reservation without leave, joined Gonshayee and several other members of the SI band, traveled north a short distance, and engaged in a tiswin party that lasted two or three days. Later, on May 31 or possibly early on the morning of June 1, Kid passed through San Carlos and rode south to the Aravaipa Canyon with his four scouts and other band members. Upon arriving in the camp of Chiquito's SA band, Kid shot and killed Rip. These feuds between bands were common, and Apache social custom accepted this as payback for the earlier killings by Rip's band. As noted earlier, in the nineteenth century, federal law sanctioned disputes that were resolved by tribal courts or councils.[17]

On the afternoon of June 1, 1887, Gonshayee, acting as a messenger, arrived at San Carlos and explained to Captain Pierce that Kid wanted to talk to him. Pierce claimed, "I told him that he could come if he pleased and that the sooner he came the better it would be for him."[18] Kid and his four scouts, Askisaylala, Bachoandoth, Nahconquisay, and Margey, returned to San Carlos and rode up in front of Al Sieber's tent; they were prepared to surrender and accept their punishment. They were accompanied by Gonshayee and about a dozen band members mounted on horses, many armed with rifles. Captain Pierce ordered Kid and the other four scouts to turn in their rifles and gun belts; they complied, placing their weapons on a table in front of the tent. Then Captain Pierce ordered them to go to the *Calaboose,* meaning the guardhouse. Kid testified at his court-martial that Antonio Díaz, the interpreter, spoke to them in Apache, and said that "all the Indians that don't obey the orders will be sent to Florida." When Díaz made this statement, he pointed "south, putting his hand and making a circle in his hand which stood for island."[19] This comment by Díaz in Apache, and the hand gesture, startled Gonshayee and his band members, who "were much excited." Kid said, "I thought those outside thought then that we Scouts would be sent down to Florida."[20] Pierce testified that "just then I heard a little noise that attracted my attention in front of the tent and I saw a few men on horseback who were bringing down their fire arms and getting cartridges from their belts. I said[,] lookout[,] Sieber[,] they are going to fire. Immediately there was a shot fired by some one in the party in front of the tent."[21] A member of Gonshayee's band, probably Miguel, fired a shot, hitting Sieber in the ankle. The five scouts fled on foot while Gonshayee's SI band members fired sev-

Gonshayee and four San Carlos SI band Apaches in Florence, Arizona, 1888.
Courtesy of the Arizona Historical Society, Tucson, AHS No. 30415.

eral more shots before quickly riding out of the agency. This series of events sparked a dual-front Apache raid into southern Arizona that would ultimately lead to shootings, a court-marshal, a trial, and a Supreme Court ruling.

THE "LAST RAID"

The Apache concept of raiding had a historical tradition that began during the fourteenth century. The Pueblo, Pima, and Papago were the first victims of these early attacks that focused on taking corn and other commodities. Later, with the intrusion of the Spanish into the Southwest, the Apaches turned their attention to stealing horses, cattle, or other possessions in their

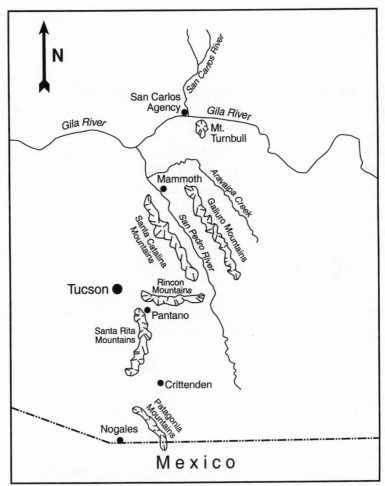

Map showing the mountainous region of southern Arizona,
site of Gonshayee's raid in 1887. *Courtesy of Melodie Tune, graphic artist,
Instructional Technology Services, San Diego State University.*

numerous raids. During the late eighteenth and early nineteenth
centuries, the Apaches increased their onslaughts, stealing thou-
sands of head of cattle and horses from the Spanish and Mexican ranchers along the northern border of Mexico. Raiding
parties were normally small, consisting of about ten or twelve
band members. The Apaches developed these raids into an

integral part of their economy. Members of the raiding party could enhance their stature within the band and also gain glory by participating in such sorties against the enemy. In his examination of the Chiricahua Apaches, Opler claims that "since raid and war are viewed as industrial pursuits, unwillingness to participate in them is attributed to indolence rather than cowardice." Apache raids were "the special interests of those who have supernatural power to find or frustrate the enemy."[22] Band chiefs were chosen for their ability to lead raiding parties and were respected only if they provided strong spiritual power and good military leadership. However, if they did not satisfy the majority, or if their tactics proved ineffective and resulted in casualties, another warrior could come forward and lead the band.[23]

Because of this fluidity, Apache band chiefs like Gonshayee held only nominal power and sometimes could not dictate or control the behavior of their clan members. Captain Pierce testified that Gonshayee "complained to me several times that he could not do any thing with them. That they would not obey him."[24]

On Thursday, June 2, seventeen Apache "renegades," some on foot, were reported to be near Mount Turnbull and heading south. By the next day, Gonshayee had split his raiding party into two groups. The first raiding party, with about ten men, and led by Gonshayee, moved southeast along the San Pedro River looking for horses. They arrived at a ranch near Mammoth Mill in the Bunker Hill Mining District the next day and, at about 3 p.m., Gonshayee, with two others, slipped in behind William Diehl, who was chopping down a tree, and shot him to death. After firing several shots at a second man who took refuge in a cabin, they quickly moved to a corral nearby and captured nine to twelve horses from Achley's ranch. They also took time to kill a mule for food, and then they headed southwest, seeking refuge in the Santa Catalina Mountains.[25] The second raiding party, led by Kid, with Sayes, Miguel, Margey, and others, crossed the Aravaipa River and moved southeast into the Galiuro Mountains, where they stopped to rest.

Three days later, on Sunday, June 5, the U.S. Army pursuit group from San Carlos, led by Second Lieutenant Carter P. Johnson of the 10th Cavalry, spotted a plume of smoke from a fire in the Santa Catalina Mountains; it was soon answered by a similar signal fire in the Galiuro Mountains, about twenty-five miles to the east. The use of smoke signals to communicate with other bands on a raid had become a common practice among many Native American groups in the American West. Opler claims that often smoke signals were used to determine whether approaching groups were "friends or foes." When "one party of men sees another in the distance, it lights a fire to the right of it and sends up one column of smoke. This means, 'Who are you?'" The other group will build a fire to answer the first.[26] An experienced officer who had worked his way up from private to lieutenant, Johnson had honed his skills hunting Apaches by helping to track down and capture Mangus in 1886.

By June 5, Lieutenant Johnson, with four Apache scouts, was rapidly following the main raiding party's trail that led from Achley's ranch toward the Santa Catalina Mountains. The second raiding party had left the Galiuro Mountains, proceeded down Sulphur Springs Valley, and then turned southwest, traveling over one hundred miles to Crittenden, a small settlement less than twenty miles north of the Mexican border. A U.S. Army dispatch reported that on Wednesday, June 8, "one or two Indians who had left the main party" had killed Michael Grace in Temporal Gulch, an isolated area in the Santa Rita Mountains about six miles southwest of Crittenden.[27] After a brief gun battle with William Leek, who lived near Grace's property, Kid's band of raiders fled southeast and had been last sighted heading for the Patagonia Mountains, less

than twelve miles away. Captain Lawton, Captain Hatfield, and
Captain Martin each had troops who were pursuing the second
raiding party.[28] These two killings by the raiders created fear
among settlers across southeastern Arizona. One newspaper
reported, the fact that the Apaches "have gone on the war path
cannot longer be doubted. By the killing of Diehl on the San
Pedro and Grace in the Santa Ritas they proclaim their bloody
mission and must be hunted to death."[29]

On Friday, June 10, Gonshayee's party, which had been traveling south from the Santa Catalina Mountains, had now
decided to turn north two miles west of Pantano, and moved
toward the Rincon Mountains to seek refuge and take a long-
needed rest. In Gonshayee's group, seven were on horseback
and four others were on foot. The next day Lieutenant Johnson
and his scouts, who had been pushing hard in pursuit, "surprised the hostile camp on top Rincon Mountains at noon."
The attack was completely unexpected, and Lieutenant Johnson
"forced them to abandon all of their horses, saddles and blankets" and compelled them to quickly scatter down the mountains on foot with only their weapons.[30] The next morning, all
signs indicated that they were moving north; they crossed the
San Pedro River and were heading back to San Carlos. Another
U.S. Army dispatch from Brigadier General Nelson A. Miles
claimed that the raiding party had "passed several herds and
unprotected ranches without committing any depredations."
The pursuing party, led by Johnson, "believe they are badly rat-
tled and worried, and anxious to get back."[31]

On Thursday, June 16, General Miles sent a dispatch stating
that "there will be no necessity for any more troops to move
further north at present." Trailing the "hostiles" north, Lieutenant Johnson "struck trail again where the Indians crossed
Aravaipa Cañon."[32] They had passed seven miles west of
Thomas, northeast near Stevens Ranch, at Eagle Creek, with
ten or more in the party. Johnson reported that they were defi-

nitely heading back to San Carlos. On Saturday morning, June 18, Ashkoelgo left Gonshayee's party and came ahead into San Carlos to surrender. After spending two days in the guardhouse, he provided information on the raiders that indicated that they were indeed shook up and wanted to give themselves up. Gonshayee and Kid wanted the troops to stop chasing them; Ashkoelgo said, "Your pressing them so close has scattered them." He claimed that if Johnson's men pulled back, they would come in of their own accord.[33] Meanwhile, the second party, led by Kid, had been "reported near Elgin," about twenty miles east of Crittenden and over a hundred miles south of San Carlos. However, Gonshayee and his party of "renegades" had been rapidly pressed by Lieutenant Johnson's troops and had been driven back to the reservation.

On Wednesday, June 22, Gonshayee rode in to San Carlos and surrendered with seven members of his band. Once again acting as a mediator, Gonshayee talked to Captain Pierce and claimed that Kid wanted to come in. The commanding officer at San Carlos informed Gonshayee that it would be best for Kid to come in immediately. This message was delivered to Kid by Gonshayee. Three days later on Saturday, June 25, the second raiding group finally arrived at San Carlos; Kid, Gonshayee, Vacasheviejo, Sayes, Miguel, Margey, and two other band members surrendered to Captain Pierce.

On Sunday, June 26, General Miles sent a dispatch reporting that Lieutenant Johnson "has driven band of hostiles back to the reservation where they have surrendered."[34] General Miles ordered an investigation and a general court-martial to try the Apache scouts who had left San Carlos. In his final report on this incident, Miles noted that, while on this raid, the Apaches killed Diehl and Grace, "which will probably be made the subject of judicial investigation by the criminal courts of the Territory."[35] Although this raid might seem minor on a scale measured by the exploits of Ulzana, Nana, or Geronimo, the consequences of the death of two white settlers and the charges of mutiny and desertion for Kid and the four other scouts would be far-reaching and momentous to Gonshayee and his SI band members.

THE COURT-MARTIAL OF KID

On June 25, Major Anson Mills, 10th Cavalry, presided over a court-martial convened to try First Sergeant Kid, Company A, Indian Scouts, charged with "mutiny, in violation of the 22nd Article of War" because he disobeyed an order of a commanding officer to go to the guardhouse. The judge advocate also charged Kid with "desertion, in violation of the 47th Article of War" because he deserted and fled from San Carlos on June 1, 1887. Lieutenant James Baldwin, acting as defense counsel, pled his client not guilty on both counts and argued that since the defendant returned to his post and surrendered voluntarily, the charge of desertion was not valid.[36] After a series of challenges to members of the court-martial panel, they finally convened.

The judge advocate called Captain F. E. Pierce to testify. Pierce claimed to have known Kid for about two years and, in April 1887, Captain P. L. Lee had enlisted Kid for a fourth stint as a scout. Pierce testified that on May 28, 1887, Kid and four other scouts had gone away without leave, deserting their posts at San Carlos. On June 1, Gonshayee, acting as a messenger, arrived at San Carlos and informed Captain Pierce that the Kid wanted to talk to him. Pierce advised Gonshayee that Kid should come in and report to him. Kid, of course, had been on a tiswin binge and had ridden to Aravaipa Canyon, where he had killed Rip to satisfy a blood feud. Oddly enough, Captain Pierce was not interested in the shooting of another Apache; it was being away without leave that concerned this army officer. Pierce claimed that Kid and the other scouts came in about sundown and were waiting in front of Al Sieber's tent. Both Pierce and Sieber walked over to meet with Kid.[37]

The judge advocate attempted to establish that the Kid was an important member of the SI band and claimed that he "was such an influential man that he had once been named for chief but would not accept and that he had such influence that he could work his will on the others."[38] When questioned about Kid's influence, Pierce testified that Kid's "Grandfather was chief of the band. The chief died last December." The band members selected Gonshayee as the new chief. Pierce stated that the band members, however, held Kid in high regard. The judge advocate asked how many days Kid had been absent from his post, and Pierce replied, "Twenty-five days including the first of June." During cross-examination, Lieutenant Baldwin asked, "Was he the popular choice for chief of his people?" Pierce responded, "He was not the popular choice." Asked whether he had a loyal following within his band, Pierce replied, "I think he has considerable influence in his band."[39] Defense asked, "Who was the medium of communication between you and the accused at this time. Answer: Gonshayee." Pierce admitted during cross-examination that the defendant did not take back his surrendered arms or commit "a hostile act, either by word, look, or movement."[40]

Asked about what happened on June 1, when Kid came in to surrender, Pierce claimed that Gonshayee, with about twenty mounted Apache horsemen, rode in and watched Kid's surrender of his arms. When Antonio Díaz, the interpreter, translated what Captain Pierce had said, there was commotion and noise among the mounted Apaches, and one or more were raising their weapons. Lieutenant Baldwin asked to whom Pierce was referring when stating they were "going to fire." Pierce replied, "To some people who were on horseback, men of his band." The first shot came from the center of the mounted horsemen, and Pierce claimed that several "shots came almost all together after the first one."[41]

The judge advocate had Al Sieber, chief of the San Carlos Apache scouts, sworn in as a witness in his own living quarters because he had been shot in the foot and was in a great deal of pain. Sieber testified that on June 1, First Sergeant Kid, who had been absent for five days without permission, had returned to San Carlos early in the evening and Captain Pierce had disarmed him and the four other scouts. Asked who were the Apaches who had accompanied Kid when he surrendered, Sieber claimed that they, along with Kid, all were members of the San Carlos SI band led by Gonshayee. Sieber said that Gonshayee's band appeared to be "war-like, I thought so by their looks, and by their having arms in their hands which is against orders here." Sieber also complained that Kid "answered me gruffly."[42] The chief of scouts claimed that after the scouts had turned in their weapons, Kid gave the other scouts a knowing look. The judge advocate asked Sieber how he interpreted that look. He replied, "Kid gave the look to these four scouts, after the captain telling them twice to go to the calaboose. I thought they had an understanding before they came in here, that if a certain thing transpired, which was ordering them to the guardhouse when they did come in, that by a look from Kid, each man knew what to, which they did in each man jumping for their arms."[43] It was clear from the testimony that Sieber was very angry with Kid, the other scouts, their behavior, and also because the wound that he suffered in the ankle would plague him for the rest of his life.

The judge advocate called Antonio Díaz, interpreter at San Carlos, for the prosecution. He testified that he was with Captain Pierce and Al Sieber when the scouts came in to surrender. Díaz asked Kid where he had been, and he replied, "We have been off and have killed a man at the Aravaipa." The witness then said to him, "I am sorry." Kid replied, "It is no matter of yours nor of the agents. It is our affair and no one else's." Díaz replied, "That is all right, it does not matter to me whether you kill ten or a dozen Indians a day, and I suppose it does not matter to the Captain either." Then he began to lecture Kid on responsibility and doing the right thing, and being aware of the consequences, especially for those scouts who had families and kids.[44] The witness claimed that while he was talking to Kid, Al Sieber came up to them and said, "Hello Kid." The scout replied hello. Captain Pierce asked them to give up their arms and Kid immediately gave up his gun. Díaz admitted that he did not see anyone else except Bachoandoth grab a gun because his attention was focused on the mounted Apaches with Gonshayee. Asked by the judge advocate who they were, he replied, "I remember particularly Miguel, a Yaqui, and Gonshayee. He had no arms." He testified that he saw Bachoandoth and Miguel fire their weapons "in the direction of the tent."[45]

Defense counsel asked Díaz how long he had been an interpreter at San Carlos. The witness replied, "About four years and eight months." Under cross-examination by Lieutenant Baldwin, the witnesses admitted that Kid said nothing when Bachoandoth claimed that they must fight. Asked whether Kid's being there was because of the killing of Rip, Díaz replied, "The Captain did not say anything to me." Díaz admitted that he "was excited when the shooting began." Counsel: "If you fell back and did not devote much attention to . . . Captain Pierce and Sieber, and then ran around the tent and ran home like a deer, how can you swear on your oath that you saw Bachoandoth shoot at Captain Pierce, and Miguel fire a shot toward the tent?"[46] He repeated his earlier testimony that Bachoandoth did get his rifle and that both he and Miguel fired at the tent.

Defense counsel then cross-examined Al Sieber in his quarters. Sieber claimed to have known Kid for about eight years. Lieutenant Baldwin asked, "Did Kid get possession of any

arms, so far as you know?" Sieber answered, "No, sir."
Counsel: "Do you understand the Apache language?" Sieber
answered, "Not thoroughly." Sieber admitted that "there was
no cry given by any of the scouts." Asked whether Kid had any
gun belts or weapons, Sieber replied, "He did not." Counsel
asked about Kid's character, and Sieber admitted that "his general character has always been good."[47]

Lieutenant Baldwin began his defense of Kid by calling Gonshayee, chief of the San Carlos SI band, as the first witness.
Gonshayee admitted that he was with a group of Apaches from
his band and that they had accompanied Kid to surrender.
When asked whether the scouts had made an "arrangement
that if the Kid was sent to the guard house that it would be
resisted," Gonshayee replied, "I don't know whether they made
any arrangement about it before they came in or not." Asked if
Kid had any arms, Gonshayee replied, "He had no arms, he
had given them up before." During cross-examination, the
judge advocate asked, "When did you see Kid again after you
saw him at the Indian hospital?" Gonshayee answered, "I saw
him afterwards way up the Gila." Asked if he had a horse, the
witness replied, "He was on foot."[48]

When defense counsel called Sayes, the judge advocate
objected because the witness had been a member of the raiding
party during the outbreak. Finally, after some discussion, Sayes
was permitted to testify. Asked where he was when Kid came in,
Sayes replied, "I was on horseback near Sieber's tent that
evening." Baldwin asked, "Was there an understanding among
the scouts or other Indians that if the scouts were sent to the
guard house that they would resist?" After objection from the
judge advocate, he was allowed to answer the question. Sayes
replied, "No sir." Counsel asked what the scouts who were
coming in intended to do. Sayes replied, "Kid said to the
scouts . . . 'We will obey orders whatever Sieber says.'" During
cross-examination, the judge advocate asked Sayes if Kid was

riding a horse or was on foot when he escaped. Sayes answered that he was "on foot." The judge advocate asked again whether Kid was on a horse, and Sayes replied, "He was not."[49]

Lieutenant Baldwin began the final stage of his defense of Kid by introducing four discharges from the U.S. Army as evidence to document the character of First Sergeant Kid as a military scout. These documents were signed by Captain Emmet Crawford, Lieutenant Britton Davis, and Lieutenant Dugan, all of the 3rd Cavalry. These papers revealed that Kid's services as a scout had been excellent.

Defense counsel stated that he had no more witnesses, but the defendant wanted to make a statement on his own behalf. The judge advocate agreed to allow him to speak. Kid stated:

> I am 1st Sergeant Kid, San Carlos, A.T. I left here without permission from Sieber or the Captain. I went up to camp and I drank a whole lot of tizwin and got back here in the night, and I passed through here, we went down to kill 'Rip' on the Aravaipa. Rip is the man who put up a job to kill my grandfather. . . . As soon as I got up to Rip's camp I saw Rip and shot him. After that I came back, I had been absent five days.

Kid thought about coming back to San Carlos and, finally, after sending Gonshayee to negotiate with Sieber, he agreed to come in and submit to any punishment by Sieber. "I told all the Scouts they must give up their arms and to obey orders." Captain Pierce arrived and told them to give up their guns and belts; they all complied. Sieber said, "Calaboose," meaning they should go to the guardhouse. Then Antonio Díaz, the interpreter, spoke roughly to them in Apache, saying "all the Indians that don't obey the orders will be sent to Florida." At the same time all the Indians [Gonshayee and his SI band members] outside made a noise and were much excited about what Antonio had spoke. I thought those outside thought then that we Scouts would be sent down to Florida. At the same time I heard a shot.[50] Several of the scouts tried to grab their weapons lying on the table, but Sieber and Pierce prevented them from getting their rifles. There were several shots fired by members of Gonshayee's band, and Kid and the four scouts fled without their arms. Kid testified, "I was on foot and went down towards the river. . . . I was without arms." He found the other scouts and members of his band up on the hill. He admitted that after leaving he did not return for about twenty-five days. Kid said, "When I was out in the mountains General Miles sent word to me that I must come back, that it would be better for me and all my people." The scout continued, "I had been obeying orders, but God sent bad spirits in my heart. I think you all know all the people can't get along very well in the world. There are some good people and some bad people amongst them all." Kid claimed that "if I had made any arrangement before I came in, I would not have given up my arms at Mr. Sieber's tent. That is all I have to say." He also admitted, "I am not educated like you and therefore can't say very much."[51]

Turning to a discussion of military rules, defense counsel asked Captain Pierce if the defendant had been instructed "in the rules and articles of war." Pierce replied, "The articles of war have never been read and translated to him to my knowledge. He has been verbally instructed in his duties as a soldier."[52] Kid, like most Apache scouts, probably had a very limited understanding of English and even less understanding of military rules.

Defense counsel then began his summation of the facts, noting that "in trying this defendant as a soldier of the United States Army we are trying him also as an Indian." Counsel continued, "This brings before us two facts. One, the Indian civilization of the nineteenth century, the other the alleged crime of Mutiny."[53] They were trying an Indian for mutiny, a charge that he did not fully understand. Baldwin noted that none of the witnesses at Sieber's tent had "implicated the defendant in a wrongful act."[54] Defense counsel noted that Kid had gone to see Sieber and was contrite about his "previous errors" and had submitted to the authority of the chief of scouts. The testimonies of Sieber and Pierce conflict. Sieber claimed the scouts tried to get their guns, but Captain Pierce testified that they did not. Further, Pierce showed no fear or concern when the scouts came up to Sieber's tent. Counsel said, "I ask would those scouts have surrendered their arms, if any prearrangement had been entered into, any signal agreed upon? No." Baldwin continued, "Had this defendant meant war . . . would he not have led the revolt?" Counsel said, "But no. He fled unarmed. He vanished from the sight of those at the tent."[55]

Lieutenant Baldwin observed, "True to the traditions of his race, at the sound of turbulent strife he fled unarmed, why, because the history of his people has taught him to scan with suspicious eye the figure of justice when a white man and an Indian is concerned." Counsel continued,

> But I may say it is fortunate for this unfortunate defendant that this court will turn from the atmosphere of prejudice which surrounds the Indian, and which will close its ear to the clamor of those who cry out for the extermination of this people because they stand in the way of the white man's greed. This defendant, a stranger to our language, unconscious of our laws, customs, and habits, and spring from a race still in the darkness of barbarism.[56]

Baldwin cautioned the court, "In crime and particularly the crime of mutiny, there is an essential element. Intent, hence from the evidence it is affirmatively shown that this defendant was only present at the outbreak, he aided not, he assisted not, he countenanced not, he abetted not, but quick to fear the white man . . . he fled unarmed."[57] Baldwin, of course, realized that one of the problems with these proceedings was that the court-martial panel was holding an Apache to the same standards of white soldiers who were educated and fluent in English. Kid had no formal education and thus could not be expected to understand all of the nuances of military law. Further, if he did not understand the language, and if the rules of military service were not translated and explained to him, he could not possibly be expected to comprehend their meaning and abide by them.

After deliberating the charges against Kid, the court-martial panel returned a verdict of guilty to both charges of mutiny and desertion and sentenced First Sergeant Kid "to suffer death by shooting with musketry, two thirds of the members of the Court having voted for this sentence."[58] The verdict was signed by Major Anson Mills, president of the panel. By order of Brigadier General Nelson Miles, the commanding general, the court-martial panel reconsidered its verdict and reduced it to life in prison. General Miles, however, further reduced the punishment to a ten-year sentence to be served at the federal prison on Alcatraz Island.

GONSHAYEE'S TRIAL

The Apaches came from a culture that white society could not comprehend, and thus, jurors were unlikely to be neutral, let alone sympathetic, to Indian defendants. Their dress, lifestyle, physical appearance, and poor English put the Apaches at great disadvantage the first day they walked into the courtroom. Gonshayee and his band members would discover the unfairness of the U.S. District Court system in Phoenix, Arizona. They were at the mercy of the whims and caprices of an unsympathetic white population that perceived Indian crime as being much worse than such behavior by members of its own community.

In the U.S. District Court in Phoenix, Maricopa County, presiding Judge William W. Porter selected H. N. Alexander and L. H. Chalmers to defend Gonshayee. On May 29, 1888, defense counsel appeared in court to defend their client, who had been charged with murder. Following the methods employed in their handling of Captain Jack's trial, Alexander and Chalmers filed a demurrer stating that the federal authorities had "no jurisdiction to hear and determine this case, nor jurisdiction of the person of the defendant." Defense counsel claimed "that the defendant is an Indian charged with killing a white man within the District, Second Judicial, naming no County or locality." Defense also called the indictment "vague and uncertain as to the locality and time" of the killing, and this would "deprive the defendant of a substantial right, viz: the defense of Alibi. The only locality named is 'within this District' (2nd Judicial) which extends over four counties." Gila, Pinal, Yuma, and Maricopa counties cover a wide region with "a radius of 300 miles." Further, the indictment alleged that the crime had been "committed 'on or about the 5th day of June 1887.'" This was too vague. They filed the demurrer with Court Clerk J. E. Walker.[59]

On May 31, 1888, the defendant appeared in court with counsel, and the court overruled the demurrer. At that point defense counsel entered a plea of not guilty. The trial began on June 4, 1888, in the U.S. District Court, Second Judicial District, in Phoenix, Arizona. Alexander and Chalmers represented Gonshayee, and Owen T. Rouse and Baker and Campbell (a local law firm) handled the prosecution for the U.S. government. U.S. District Attorney Rouse called John Scanlan to testify for the prosecution. Scanlan testified that he and William Diehl, the victim of the killing, had lived in the Bunker Hill Mining District, Pinal County. On June 3, 1887, a group of Apaches sneaked in behind Diehl and shot him; Scanlan said he heard three shots and ran for his gun. By the time he returned, three or four Apaches were running off with their horses. He found Diehl lying dead with "two bullet holes in him." The victim had been chopping down a tree prior to the shooting. Diehl's place was located about two miles east of the San Pedro River. The witness claimed that he saw about "fourteen or fifteen" Apaches. They had approached the ranch from the north, near Achley's corral, where they ran off with about eleven horses. Scanlan was unable to identify the defendant as being at the crime scene. During cross-examination, Scanlan placed the Aravaipa Creek about twelve miles east of the crime scene. Achley's corral is located about two to three miles north of Diehl's place. After the shooting, the Apaches fled south, crossed the San Pedro River, and moved into the Santa Catalina Mountains.[60]

Two individuals, J. M. Montoya and Antonio Díaz, were sworn in to translate from English to Spanish, from Spanish to Apache, and also from Apache to Spanish to English. If this sounds confusing, one can probably imagine the problems involved in keeping the translations accurate.

The prosecution called Vacasheviejo, a member of Gonshayee's band, to testify. Asked if he knew "what an oath is," the witness responded that he had no understanding of the concept of an oath. After a series of questions by defense counsel Alexander and U.S. Attorney Rouse that failed to provide any understanding, Judge William W. Porter interceded: "Ask him this question: Does he know he will be punished by the laws here if he does not tell the truth here?" The witness replied that "he understands that if he tells a lie he will be punished."[61] The witness admitted that he was a member of Gonshayee's band and had left San Carlos on June 1, 1887. The raiding party included Gonshayee, Kid, Miguel, Sayes, Nahconquisay, Askisaylala, nine other band members, and one woman. The night after Al Sieber had been shot, they rode east to some mountains, and the next day they stole a horse, "crossed and went to the Aravaipa," and killed a cow. The raiding party moved south, crossed the Galiuro Mountains, and while looking for horses, came across William Diehl's camp near Mammoth. Gonshayee, Askisaylala, and Nahconquisay headed for the ranch house while the rest hid themselves, and very soon Vacasheviejo heard gunfire. Asked if he knew anything about the killing of Diehl, the witness said he heard shooting and, when the three returned, "Gonshayee himself said that he had killed a man with a pistol."[62] After the killing, another white man began to shoot at the Apaches from the cabin. The raiding party rode off quickly and moved south toward the Santa Catalina Mountains. The witness claimed that it "might be four miles" from the ranch to the San Pedro River. Asked when they returned to San Carlos, Vacasheviejo replied, "Gonshayee came to the Reservation 22 days after; he, himself [Vacasheviejo], came 24 days after."[63]

During cross-examination, when Alexander asked why Gonshayee had killed Diehl, the witness said he did not know why. Alexander: "Ask him if they had a war dance after they killed him." The witness replied no, "they didn't have any dance."[64] Asked whether Gonshayee had personally told him the story of the killing, the witness replied no, the defendant had been talking to other Apaches while they were in jail. Asked why he did not try to stop him, Vacasheviejo claimed that he was about the lowest in rank in Gonshayee's band and, since he was the chief, nothing could be done to prevent the killing. The witness said he was about a mile and a half from the shooting and heard the shots being fired. After more questioning, the witness recanted his earlier story about how he found out about the killing; he stated that "Gonshayee himself said so—told him so."[65]

Bashlalah, called to testify, stated he was a member of the defendant's band and was present when the shooting took place. They crossed a series of hills and came upon a ranch where Nahconquisay and Askisaylala accompanied the defendant. The victim, wearing a red shirt, was chopping on an oak tree. The witness heard two shots. Gonshayee never told him what happened, but he heard that someone had killed the white man but did not know who did it. The shooting occurred on the east side of the San Pedro River. During cross-examination, he admitted that he did not see the killing of the white man and that "Gonshayee did not tell him" what had happened at the ranch.[66] Sayes, another Apache member of the raiding party, claimed that Gonshayee "said that he himself had killed the man." During cross-examination, the witness admitted that he did not see the killing.[67]

Court interpreter Antonio Díaz, was sworn in as a witness and was examined by the prosecution. He claimed that he was at San Carlos when Al Sieber was shot and testified that the defendant was one of those Apaches involved who left the reservation on June 1, 1887. Díaz claimed that "Gonshayee said there before the Commissioner [at Tucson] that he himself and three more of his men went down to kill the man; one of the party loaned him his rifle; all four went down and shot at the man and killed him."[68] After this testimony, U.S. District Attorney Rouse closed testimony against the defendant. Oddly enough, Alexander and Chalmers, counsel for the defense, informed the judge that they would call "no witnesses for the defense."[69] The judge closed testimony, the prosecution gave its final arguments, and then the judge began to give his instructions to the jury.

The entire trial lasted less than one day, and after a very brief deliberation the jury returned to the courtroom, where Charles A. Boake, jury foreman, handed the verdict to the judge. The court clerk read the verdict, which pronounced "the defendant guilty of murder as charged in the indictment."[70] To conduct a trial, complete with jury deliberation, within one day suggests that the Apache defendants could hardly have been given a fair hearing. Gonshayee and other defendants were at the mercy of an unfair criminal justice system.[71] Nevertheless, Judge William W. Porter accepted the verdict and adjourned until the next day. On June 5, 1888, defense counsel filed a "Motion in Arrest of Judgment." Defense counsel argued that the grand jury had no legal authority to charge the defendant with murder. According to the defense's argument, the federal court that ordered and summoned the grand jury had no jurisdiction in this case. Defense claimed that the alleged crime had not been committed in Maricopa County, where the court convened. Moreover, "that the Court which ordered the Grand Jury summoned and which tried the case" was a federal court in the Second Judicial District of Arizona Territory, which had no jurisdiction over this case. Further, the indictment did not conform to the Penal Code of Arizona Territory. Finally, "the indictment is so vague and uncertain as to time and place; that the defendant was deprived of a substantial right."[72] On June 12, Judge Porter ruled against the defense motion. Two days later, Gonshayee appeared with counsel Alexander and Chalmers for his final sentencing. Asked if he had "any legal cause to show why judgment should not be pronounced," defense counsel replied no. Judge Porter ordered that

Gonshayee be removed hence to the County Jail of Maricopa County or other place of secure confinement and there be securely kept until Friday the 10th day of August, a.d. 1888, and on that day you be taken by the United States Marshal of the Territory of Arizona, to and within the yard of the jail of said Maricopa County, Arizona, between the hours of nine o'clock a.m. and five o'clock p.m. of that day, by said Marshal you be hanged by the neck till you are dead.[73]

On the day of the sentence, defense counsel filed a "Notice of Appeal" to the Supreme Court of the Territory of Arizona.[74] This set in motion a legal battle that ended in the U.S. Supreme Court and eventually included ten other cases involving Apaches prosecuted in Arizona Territory in 1887 and 1888.

Gonshayee, convicted of murder in this case, gained legal fame by appealing his conviction to the U.S. Supreme Court. The Arizona territorial criminal justice system, as well as other legal systems throughout the United States, failed to provide any method for bringing the American Indian into this new, complicated, and alien legal system. How could an Apache possibly understand the complicated legal concepts? Gonshayee did not speak the English language, he was unaware of his legal rights, he could not comprehend how the system worked, and he did not receive good legal counsel.[75] These Native Americans committed acts that were accepted as normal behavior by Apache standards, but those same acts were perceived differently by white society.

There were two cultures, one dominated by a complex system of legal control, the other centered on social control dictated by several hundred years of tribal traditions. One could not expect Native Americans to adjust to this new system without adequate guidance and training; however, there was no attempt to educate the Apaches on the various nuances of criminal justice. To add to this confusion, in terms of violent crime, Arizona Territory had a joint control system with powers shared in various jurisdictions. Originally, the federal district courts ruled over criminal cases that occurred on federal military posts and Indian reservations, but their jurisdiction over the other territorial land was rather vague and undetermined.

In 1885 Congress enacted the Major Crimes Act as an amendment to the Indian appropriations bill. Section nine of the Indian Appropriations Act of March 3, 1885, placed a series of major crimes under the control of the federal and territorial governments. The law stated that "all Indians, committing against the person or property of another Indian or other person . . . murder, manslaughter, rape, assault with intent to kill, arson, burglary, and larceny within any Territory of the United States, and either within or without an Indian reservation, shall be subject" to the laws of that territory and will be tried "as are all other persons charged with the commission of such crimes." Further, all Indians that commit any of these crimes within "any State of the United States, and within the limits of any Indian reservation, shall be subject to the same laws, tried in the same courts and in the same manner, and subject to the same penalties as are all other persons committing any of the above crimes within the exclusive jurisdiction of the United States."[76]

By passing the Major Crimes Act, Congress sharply curtailed tribal sovereignty and increased federal and territorial governmental control, which extended onto Indian reservations. Crimes committed by Indians on reservations or regions nearby were now placed under the federal and territorial criminal justice systems. The first challenge to the Major Crimes Act came with *U.S. v. Kagama*. The U.S. Supreme Court held that "the nature of the offense [murder] is one which in most all cases of its commission is punishable by the laws of the states, and within the jurisdiction of their courts." The court concluded that the "Indian tribes *are* the wards of the nation. They are communities *dependent* on the United States."[77] The U.S. Supreme Court ruled that Congress had a right to pass the Major Crimes Act of 1885 to control behavior on Indian reservations and that it "is a valid law in both its branches, and that the circuit court of the United States for the district of California has jurisdiction of the offense charged in the indictment in this case."[78] This decision clarified criminal jurisdiction.

Clearly, the Major Crimes Act placed seven major crimes (including homicide) that occurred on Indian reservations under the jurisdiction of federal courts.

EX PARTE GONSHAYEE

In May 1888, during Gonshayee's trial, two Apache witnesses stated that the defendant admitted to them that he had indeed killed William Diehl, a white man, south of San Carlos near Mammoth, in Pinal County. After hearing the testimony, the jury deliberated briefly and found Gonshayee guilty of murder, and according to federal law section 5339, the judge sentenced him to death.[79] A careful reading of the short, twenty-five-page court transcript strongly suggests that Gonshayee committed the crime. The question of evidence, however, was not important in this case, which was appealed to the U.S. Supreme Court. In their appeal, legal counsel claimed that the U.S. District Court, under which the proceedings occurred, did not have jurisdiction over this case, as dictated by the Major Crimes Act of 1885. Defense counsel asked for a writ of habeas corpus. The court agreed to hear the petitioners.

In a case that held important implications for several similar Indian homicide cases in Arizona Territory, Justice Samuel F. Miller carefully cited *Ex Parte Crow Dog*, the Major Crimes Act of 1885, and *U.S. v. Kagama.* Justice Miller noted that controversy revolved around whether Gonshayee's crime "was an offense against the laws of the United States . . . or whether it was an offense against the laws of the territory and should have been tried under those laws."[80] Although the indictment did not cite specifically where the crime occurred, there was no doubt that Diehl had been killed in Pinal County. The Court observed that the legal proceedings had been conducted in Phoenix, Maricopa County, and that the prosecutor, grand jury, petit jury, and marshal all represented the U.S. Second District Court in Arizona Territory. The question remained: did the federal court or the territorial county court have jurisdiction? The U.S. Supreme Court ruled that the law was quite clear—original jurisdiction resided in the territorial courts of Arizona. In this case, the territorial court system in Pinal County should have tried Gonshayee.[81]

Although the five U.S. District Courts held their sessions within the county seats of five counties, and used the same judges as the county courts, they still needed to be separated, because they were distinctively different. The Pinal County sheriff should have secured Gonshayee, the defendant; the county grand jury should have issued the indictment; the county district attorney should have prosecuted the defendant; and the county judge should have heard the case. By assuming jurisdiction over the case, the U.S. District Court had exceeded its powers. Justice Miller well understood that federal law dealing with homicide only recognized first-degree murder, which called for the death penalty. One can understand, then, why the Supreme Court justice suggested that the defendant was entitled to the same trial as others in the various county jurisdictions that recognized first- and second-degree murder.[82] Justice Miller noted that

> the Indian shall at least have all the advantages which may accrue from that change [Major Crimes Act], which transfers him, as to the punishment for these crimes, from the jurisdiction of his own tribe to the jurisdiction of the government of the Territory in which he lives.[83]

The Supreme Court issued the writ to release the defendant.

U.S. v. Gonshayee had important implications. It was followed by *U.S. v. Captain Jack,* and these two cases brought the

eventual release of eleven Apache Indians convicted of murder
or attempted murder in U.S. District Courts. The U.S. Supreme
Court sent all of these cases down to the Arizona Territorial
Supreme Court, which, in turn, reversed the convictions and
sent them to the county courts. Nevertheless, overturning the
convictions did not ensure that the defendants would go free.
All of the Apache defendants under this decision, except Captain Jack, were retried in the county courts and found guilty.

FINAL OBSERVATIONS

With legal jurisdiction over the Gonshayee case resolved, in
1889 Pinal County authorities prosecuted Gonshayee and seven
other Apaches for murder.[84] Unfortunately, only a few newspaper stories are available to describe what happened to the
defendants; all of the criminal case files have mysteriously disappeared. Similarly, the coroner's inquest on William Diehl's
body also has vanished. On October 19, 1889, the local newspaper in Florence, Pinal County, reported that Gonshayee, Askisaylala, and Nahconquisay had been convicted for the murder
of William Diehl and had been sentenced to be hanged.[85] The
Arizona newspaper reporter noted that "the halter is very close
to the necks of the five Apache Indians" who were convicted of
murder. The reporter claimed that "one of the slayers of Diehl
recited the details of the killing in a horribly brutal and boastful
way. He told how he sighted his victim from the rocks above
and what a splendid shot he made with a pistol, and laughed
with fiendish glee at the hellish crime." The reporter claimed
that "they were all given a fair and impartial trial."[86] A newspaper editor, who had carried on a long tradition of vilifying
Apaches, observed that "Florence will soon have a hanging
picnic of five Apaches . . . a step in the right direction. If the
civil authorities had dealt with these 'Red Devils' all along since

Arizona became a Territory, the Apache troubles would have been quelled long before they were."[87] Finally, the Florence newspaper's editor observed, "It is safe to say that should a few bands of Apaches be taken from the war path and suspended by their necks, where the other Indians on the reservation could get a good, fair look at them, there would be no more Apache outbreaks."[88]

What actually happened in the courtroom remains a mystery. Judge W. H. Barnes, District Court, Second Judicial District, presided over the case (No. 35), but there are no indictments, subpoenas, jury lists, witnesses, trial notes, or prosecutor's notes extant. No doubt it was a trial of short duration with an all-white jury, but otherwise we can only conjecture about what actually took place in the courtroom. What we do know is that the Pinal County District Court quickly retried, convicted, and sentenced Gonshayee and seven other Apaches to death by hanging.

Looking back, the results of this case study should not be too surprising. The "last raid" conducted by Gonshayee's band, which included two white victims, ensured that the government would prosecute the offending parties. Ironically, it was considered acceptable to kill another Apache, but not white settlers, in Arizona Territory. Considering the animosity held by white settlers and soldiers toward the Apaches, this inconsistent prosecution of the defendants should be expected. The Apaches had to conform to the social norms of their white conquerors, who viewed them as the enemy; therefore, they would be prosecuted to the fullest extent. It had become a strange, alien, and hostile world for the Apaches. It was, indeed, the "last raid" for Gonshayee and his band.

CHAPTER 3

BETWIXT AND BETWEEN

The "Carlisle Kid"

What did you put my father in the jail for? Now, you want
to put me in jail too? You will not put me in jail.

NAHDEIZAZ,

U.S. v. Nahdeizaz, May 11, 1887

ON MARCH 10, 1887, Nahdeizaz, a young Tonto Apache,
rode up beside Lieutenant Seward Mott at the San Carlos
Agency, argued angrily with him, pulled a Colt revolver, and
shot and killed the officer. A few years later, on January 8,
1891, Plenty Horses, a Brulé Sioux warrior, shot Lieutenant
Edward W. Casey. Though different in some respects, these
cases share some intriguing commonalities. Mott, a recent
West Point graduate with no Indian experience, had just been
assigned to San Carlos. On the morning of the shooting he
had ordered the arrest of Nahdeizaz's father and placed him in
the San Carlos guardhouse. Nahdeizaz, recently returned from
Carlisle Indian School and apparently frustrated by the arrogant, overbearing attitude of Mott, confronted him and
demanded to know why his father had been jailed. After a
brief, hot argument, Nahdeizaz pulled a revolver, fired several

shots, and left his victim dying in great agony with three wounds.

In the second killing, Lieutenant Casey, a veteran officer with two decades' experience and extensive background dealing with Native Americans, had done nothing; he was simply in the wrong place at the wrong time. Plenty Horses had also recently returned from Carlisle, found himself unaccepted by his own people, and witnessed the terrible, bloody results of the Wounded Knee massacre at Pine Ridge Reservation. Filled with anger, after a chance meeting on an isolated road, Plenty Horses rode up alongside Lieutenant Casey, conversed with him in English for a few minutes, pulled up his rifle, and shot the officer in the back of the head in retaliation for Wounded Knee.

These two senseless killings share a common thread: both Native Americans had attended Carlisle Indian School and had returned to their respective reservations to discover that they had been thrust into an "unredeemable" world betwixt and between two cultures that did not accept them. Both cases ended in tragedy for the participants; however, because of various legal issues, these homicide cases turned in two very divergent directions. This case study will focus on Nahdeizaz, the Carlisle experience, the conditions at San Carlos, and the legal ramifications of Nahdeizaz's case. It can be compared to Plenty Horses's story, to trace a line between one man living a nightmare between two worlds and another convicted and incarcerated for his crime.

CARLISLE INDIAN SCHOOL

Captain Richard Henry Pratt, sometimes called the "red man's Moses," proved to be the driving force for the movement to educate and "civilize" the Native Americans, especially those in the American West. In 1879, with the support of Carl Schurz, secretary of the interior, Pratt received permission from the U.S. Army to use Carlisle Barracks in Carlisle, Pennsylvania. Pratt, a thirty-nine-year-old veteran army officer, with the support of the Friends of the Indians, the Mohonk Conference, and religious organizations, began to operate the Carlisle Indian School with the full intention of completely assimilating Native Americans into American society. He developed three principles at Carlisle Indian School: educate the Indian students "away from their native environment," teach useful technical trades and agricultural skills, and make sure that they were not returned "permanently to their tribes."[1] Pratt focused on removing the Indian children from the reservation, stripping them of their culture, and turning them into "civilized" citizens equipped to function within the white-dominated society. These principles and the physical distance from the reservations led Pratt's and similar schools to be called "away school."

To show the "effects" of Carlisle and its program, Pratt had his staff take "before and after" photographs of the students. Historian Jacqueline Fear-Segal observed that "These carefully doctored pictures were printed in pairs. The first showed dirty, unkempt, slovenly tribesmen, wearing long hair, blankets, and moccasins. The second presented the same group, dramatically transformed into scrubbed, brushed, uniformed individuals with short, parted hair, clean pressed clothes, polished books and open faces."[2] This sort of imagery, of course, impressed Carlisle visitors, who might give donations to Pratt, to "civilize" other Indian students, and to congressmen, who would be more inclined to provide funds for this educational process. His methods, though well accepted by most whites, proved to be very destructive to young Native American children, who became isolated from their families and their normal social life.

The first attempt at "civilizing" Indian students began on October 6, 1879, when Pratt and a group of Sioux children arrived at Carlisle. One white observer noted: "They were a wild outfit—badly clothed, dirty and unkempt, and altogether bearing the impression of being uncivilized." Pratt ordered his staff to take away their native dress, have them bathe, issue them uniforms, cut their hair, and, finally, select a "new name" that would identify them as becoming "civilized."[3] By November 1, Pratt's student body had swelled to about 147 and continued to grow despite his difficulty in getting government funding for the school.

Although Pratt opposed allowing his students to return to their families on the reservations, that is exactly what happened to most of them. The final results of his educational program proved to be a personal and cultural disaster for the children. Historian Oliver La Farge claimed, "Carlisle Indian School was in Pennsylvania for a purpose of inspired and brutal benevolence. Indians of high-school age were taken—often almost literally kidnapped—from the Western reservations and sent there, to remain for four, six or even more years."[4] As La Farge suggests, the process, of course, proved to be destructive and failed to "make them over into white men." It was a culture-shattering experience that returned alienated, sometimes angry, young Indians to their families to brood and, in many cases, to fail to readjust to reservation life. Even though "over four thousand Indians had attended Carlisle," the school only recognized about six hundred graduates.[5]

Pratt had strong views about the importance of changing Indian students through his regimented system at Carlisle. He claimed that "properly fed, clothed, and well taught, and as much industrially as possible, would in four years send the children into a new life and destroy savagery in this country."[6] Pratt promoted his "outing" system (sending students to work for farm families in Pennsylvania) by pushing the good results reported by some of the families who had used the students for farm labor and domestic help. You do not, however, see or hear the negative side of these outings: Indian students sometimes refused to work or were lazy and uncooperative.[7]

Pratt emphasized training the Indian students in industrial and domestic areas; Carlisle turned out graduates who had developed limited skills as carpenters, harness makers, farmers, and domestic servants. Students were not always cooperative at Carlisle. An employee at the school noted that "the discipline of the boys was pretty severe, along army rules to a large extent." Pratt's detractors perceived his attitude to be "harsh, arrogant, arbitrary," and his use of corporal punishment also received criticism.[8] One historian noted: "The devastating effect of his program upon clan and tribe seems not to have seriously disturbed" Pratt. Other critics decried his outing system and its effect. One Indian agent claimed that "these returned students are the worst Indians we have."[9] Throughout the entire period of educating Native Americans, the directors of Carlisle and other Indian schools neither asked for nor considered accepting the input of Native American leaders. Everything was developed and operated on white terms; an Indian voice would not be heard. The United States "had engulfed them. Divided by over 500 tribal affiliations . . . their voices were inaudible."[10]

Apache Students at Carlisle

During the school's early years, few Apaches attended Carlisle. In 1880, Pratt reported that Reverend Sheldon Jackson had brought one Apache and ten Pueblo children.[11] The following year, Carlisle received two new male and two new female Apache students. In early 1884, however, Pratt received fifty-two new Apache students from San Carlos. He claimed that the Apache students "proved exceptionally industrious, dutiful, and apt."[12] Although little is known about Nahdeizaz's time at Carlisle, he was probably in this group of Apache students. In 1887, Pratt reported that two Apache males were returned to

San Carlos Reservation. The exact date is unknown, but it might have been in late winter or in the spring, 1886–1887. Since other sources claim that Nahdeizaz had just returned to San Carlos prior to the shooting, he most likely was one of these two men. Pratt's report indicates that thirty-six of the forty-five Apache boys were being trained in farming.[13]

The following year, Pratt noted that "the mortality of the year was abnormally large, being 21 out of a total population of 637. Sixteen of these, 9 males and 7 females were Apaches." He reported that "all the deaths were from tubercular consumption."[14] That would be a 10.5 percent death rate from the total Apache student body at Carlisle Indian School. Asa Daklugie, a Chiricahua Apache student and the son of Juh, an important chief, provided some personal experience after visiting Carlisle's hospital. He went to visit Jasper Kanseah, who had become ill with what must have been consumption. Daklugie remembered that Kanseah said, "I am not going to die." Giving his reasoning, he said, "I don't take that medicine," explaining that "I pretend to swallow it but I don't. I hide it and I will live." Daklugie complained that the hospital was a terrible place and that "nearly every Apache taken there had died." He reported that "when one of the Apaches took that sickness [consumption] they didn't want him to die at Carlisle. They sent him to his family. . . . That is what happened to many."[15]

In 1889, once again Pratt reported high mortality rates, with eighteen deaths, of which fourteen were Apaches. All died of consumption. Despite these numbers, Pratt claimed that the sanitary conditions at Carlisle were good, and he furnished the students with a healthy, varied diet.[16] These high mortality rates indicate that Native Americans, especially Apaches, were at risk when held within a student body of over six hundred students who could be carriers of a variety of diseases. Pratt was well aware that the Apaches seemed to be more susceptible to tuberculosis, yet he "continued to recruit prospective students from among the Chiricahua prisoners, disregarding the medical danger" that could cause many deaths among these vulnerable children.[17] In May 1889, he reported to the commissioner of Indian affairs that "in the winter and spring of 1886–87, twenty-seven [Chiricahua Apaches] have died and two others will die within two or three days."[18] In each case, the cause of death was attributed to tuberculosis.

The methods of enlisting students for Carlisle are provocative. Jason Betzinez, a member of Geronimo's Chiricahua band, became one of about sixty-two Apache children recruited by Pratt in 1886. Imprisoned at Saint Augustine, Florida, Betzinez remembered how Pratt called for volunteers among the children to hold up their hands to be selected for Carlisle. When no one volunteered, Pratt "went down the line choosing forty-nine boys and girls" for Carlisle. In his later years, Betzinez recalled "when Captain Pratt came to me he stopped, looked me up and down, and smiled. I only scowled; I didn't want to go at all."[19] Betzinez would spend nine years at Carlisle Indian School.

Similar to the Sioux, the Apache children arrived at Carlisle "complete with blankets and beads, they were subjected to an almost shattering reorientation. Off came the blankets and the braids of hair."[20] Asa Daklugie also had been "recruited" and sent to Carlisle. He recalled bitterly what happened after they arrived at the school. "The next day the torture began. The first thing they did was cut our hair." He complained, "I lost my hair. And without it how would Ussen recognize me when I went to the Happy Place?" While they were being given a bath, their "breechcloths were taken," and they had to put on trousers. He complained bitterly that "we'd lost our identity as Indians. Greater punishment could hardly have been devised." Next the Apaches were taken into a room where a man went down the line, giving them names, "Asa, Benjamin, Charles, Daniel," and so forth. He started with Daklugie, since he was the son of a chief; consequently, he "became Asa Daklugie." He claimed, "I've always hated that name. It was forced on me as though I had been an animal."[21]

Unlike most Carlisle Indian School graduates, Jason Betzinez formed a very different and more positive perception of his years at school. Years later, he reminisced about his first day at Carlisle, "As I look today at our first photographs I realize what unkempt and wild-looking creatures we were." He also remembered, when they were issued army-type uniforms, that "we wore these uniforms proudly. Never before had I owned such fine-looking clothing." Finally, Betzinez felt that his "introduction to the teachings of Christianity" proved to be the "most powerful influence on" his life.[22]

Returned Students

After completing their schooling at Carlisle Indian School, the Apache students usually returned home to their reservation to live. Returning to San Carlos was fraught with all kinds of pitfalls because people around the returning students viewed them with suspicion, especially when the returning students were unable to converse in their native language and now perceived traditional methods of living in a different light. For example, some returnees could not imagine living in wickiups after their taste of the lifestyle practiced at Carlisle. Because of the new language barrier and their preferred lifestyle, the returned students had difficulty relating to their parents and relatives. Historian Michael Coleman observed that most of the students returned "with a sense of cultural and indeed personal superiority" that caused resentment in family and friends on the reservation. Most important, "many returnees soon discovered that the knowledge, skills, and trades" learned at Carlisle "were often irrelevant on the reservation."[23] Those with some training in a trade discovered there were few wagons or buggies to be repaired and little work available for harness making and horse shoeing. On the reservation such jobs were already taken by white employees, and any new jobs that opened in the trades were quickly awarded to other prospective whites.

Young men trained in farming at Carlisle found out that they "could not grow young plants in dry, wind-beaten, and worm-infested sand drifts." At San Carlos, the land proved to be unproductive, especially without adequate irrigation. Young Apache men were unable to gain employment at San Carlos. Chris, a young Mescalero Apache who attended Carlisle, complained, "The white man's got in the lead of them, and when they want jobs as mechanics or with the cattle they can't get them."[24] Some Apache men, like Jason Betzinez, who had become proficient in English, were able to gain jobs as interpreters. After reviewing studies by scholars who had interviewed young Native American students from Carlisle, historian Michael Coleman discovered that the student narrators had significant diversity of opinion, which he examined to discover how they had adjusted upon returning to the reservation. Some adjusted fairly well; others did not, and sometimes became alienated to both white and Indian culture. He found that young returnees "were often caught between cultures, without a firm grounding in either, that they were what anthropologists call 'marginal' men and women, at peace in neither world." For example, Lame Deer claimed that "the schools leave a scar. We enter them confused and bewildered and we leave them the same way."[25]

In 1884, San Carlos Indian Agent P. P. Wilcox reported that "during the year four pupils have returned from Hampton school" (another school that trained Indian students) to live on the reservation. He disclosed that "Tolma and Stagon, have enlisted as military scouts." Two other young men, Robert McIntosh and William Roberts, received employment at the agency as interpreters. Reflecting the view of most whites dealing with Indians, Wilcox complained bitterly that most of them "have purchased squaws and returned to the habits of their people. To be married to a squaw signifies an abandon-

ment of the refinements of civilization." Displaying the attitudes of Pratt, the Indian agent criticized the process of
returning the students to the reservation and suggested that
"boys taken from the tribe should remain at school until they
have mastered the trades in which they are instructed."[26]

In October 1885, Captain F. E. Pierce, Indian agent at San
Carlos, testified before a congressional committee about
Apache behavior at the reservation. Pierce had considerable
experience with Indians (more than eight years) prior to being
put in charge of San Carlos. He reported that "there are forty
boys and five girls at school at Carlisle. I think[,] in all[,] five of
that number have returned." Since their return one had died,
another had become a scout, another had been working in car-
pentry, one in the harness room, and "the other one is now
living up the San Carlos with a squaw. . . . He is the brightest
one of the lot." Pierce complained that, since marrying the
Apache woman, he had changed his habits. Asked if he was
progressing, Pierce answered, "I do not think so." Another
question: "He has gone back to the habits of his people?"
Pierce: "Very nearly so." Captain Pierce recommended, "I think
it would be better to educate them on the reservation."[27] This
last comment, of course, went against the grain of educational
thinking that wanted to take them away from the reservation to
prevent them from being "corrupted" by tribal lifestyle. The
disastrous effects of Carlisle and other away schools could best
be seen in what happened to the returned students. Pratt and
other educators received a great deal of criticism on this issue.
In an examination of the away school weaknesses, one investigator concluded, "To uproot a child from his natural environment without making any effort to teach him how to adjust
himself to a new environment, and then send him back to the
old . . . is to invite disaster."[28]

SAN CARLOS

In order to understand how Nahdeizaz and other former Carlisle school students reacted upon their return, it's important to know as much as possible about the conditions at San Carlos. As with much of what has been reported before, there are conflicting and contradictory reports, even from the same person.

In the early 1870s, General George Crook waged punitive campaigns against Yavapais, Tontos, Coyoteros, and Mohaves in the Rio Verde Valley, situated east of Prescott and below Flagstaff. They had been labeled as the most "hostile, depredating" and predatory Apaches in the Mogollon Rim country. By 1873, Crook had defeated them and confined 629 Tonto Apaches to the Camp Verde Reservation. Despite being placed on the reservation, the Tontos and Yavapais still proved troublesome, especially Delchea, a chief who was considered to be "one of the worst and most inveterate enemies" of whites in Arizona Territory.[29] On April 23, 1875, the secretary of the interior signed an order that abolished Camp Verde. Soon after, Nahdeizaz and his family, along with over a thousand Tontos, Yavapais, Coyoteros, and Mohaves, were relocated to the San Carlos Agency.[30] A few months later, a large group of Cibicue and White Mountain Apaches were also relocated there. Within one year, the Apache population at San Carlos had grown from around one thousand to more than four thousand, with many of them placed in close confinement with rival bands. One observer noted that placing so many different bands together "certainly [was] not conducive to harmony."[31]

Situated in Gila County, mountain ranges surrounded San Carlos, with Mount Turnbull dominating on the south and the Pinals toward the west. The agency buildings were on a bluff about forty-five feet above the Gila River. Because of the lack of water, the mesa was "barren of trees for shade," and the natural vegetation was sparse. One Indian agent observed that the agency buildings were located "near the edge of the mesa and are of adobes with shingle roofs."[32] Typically, the Indian agents at San Carlos, and other reservations as well, complained about the poor conditions that existed because of the lack of government funding. As a result, little could be done to improve the buildings or surrounding land.

The Apaches began to farm land on the north bank of the Gila River and also along the San Carlos River, north toward Peridot. But by 1877, government officials had relocated an additional four hundred Chiricahuas to San Carlos, bringing the total to more than five thousand resettled Apaches.

Commissioner of Indian affairs, J. C. Tiffany, usually put a positive spin on the progress of "civilizing" the Apaches at San Carlos. For example, his 1880 report claimed that they had become inclined to agriculture and were constructing irrigation ditches and had developed small fields of grain. The agent also claimed that they were ready to have their children educated and had been repeatedly asking for the establishment of a school on the reservation. A few lines later, however, he complained that the Apaches "are becoming discouraged with the slight success which has followed their own undirected and unskillful attempts to open ditches" for irrigating their fields.[33]

In another 1880 dispatch, Tiffany described the land around the San Carlos Agency and claimed that agriculture could not be satisfactorily pursued without the development of dams and irrigation ditches. He also reported that the performance of the San Carlos Police and their ability to deal with minor crime on the reservation indicated signs of progress.[34] Tiffany sometimes issued glowing reports indicating progress in farming. For example, he claimed that farm production had increased because of the development of "at least 25 miles of new irrigating ditches" constructed by the Apaches. However, the conditions that existed at San Carlos suggest that these numbers were inflated.[35] Most of the Apaches cultivated patches that ranged from only five to thirty acres.

Farming may have actually increased the Apache habit of holding tiswin drinking parties, which often led to the deaths of one or more of the revelers.[36] Throughout the nineteenth century, tiswin continued to plague the reservation, provoking quarrels and killings among the Apaches who participated in drinking parties. In 1886, Captain Pierce remonstrated that the Apaches "here are all partly civilized; that is, they dwell in rude houses and to a certain extent wear citizens' clothing. They have peculiar religious beliefs and superstitions, and their doctors or priests have great influence." Nevertheless, he reported that there was no difficulty in recruiting Apache scouts. There were 125 functioning as the San Carlos Police, and they received "$13 per month and $12 for use" of their horses. With such generous financial inducements, it was easy "to enlist on account of the pay, excitement, and opportunities of seeing new and strange countries."[37] In spite of these opportunities, two years later Captain John L. Bullis, acting Indian agent, complained that "there are still quite a number of them [Apache men] indisposed to hard work, and of a restless, roving, turbulent, and rebellious character." Bullis also reported that "there are only eight families of Indians occupying dwelling-houses on the reservation. The remainder dwell in brush houses" known as wickiups. He was encouraged, however, because many of the Apaches were wearing "some civilized garments," while others dressed "in full modern apparel."[38] In 1886, just before Nahdeizaz returned, there were 3,097 Apaches confined at the San Carlos Agency. Captain Pierce complained that there still was "no school in operation on the reservation"; however, there were preparations "to open a boarding-school" that would accommodate fifty boys. Nevertheless, Pierce was satisfied with the progress being made at San Carlos.

Not everyone shared this positive assessment. For example,

in an article discussing the San Carlos Agency, a newspaper editor noted that "the bucks are naturally the laziest beings on earth . . . and they will often suffer imprisonment in the guard house, in shackles, rather than perform the tasks" assigned to them in the fields along the Gila River.[39] Asa Daklugie, a Chiricahua Apache, also had harsh words for the conditions that existed at the agency. "San Carlos! That was the worst place in all the great territory stolen from the Apaches. . . . Where there is no grass there is no game." And, of course, "the heat was terrible."[40] Nahdeizaz returned to these somewhat unsettling surroundings in early 1887.

THE KILLING

Seward Mott, born in Mechanicville, New York, August 21, 1861, entered West Point, and graduated on June 13, 1885. On July 6, 1886, he was appointed Second Lieutenant and assigned to the 10th U.S. Cavalry at San Carlos Agency. He arrived at the reservation with D Troop around November 30, 1886. Mott received an appointment as acting ordinance officer, and on December 20, he was officially assigned as adjutant commanding Company A of the Indian Scouts.[41] This was an important command position that put him in charge of the Indian police, who dealt with petty crime, tiswin drinking parties, land disputes, and the control of Apache Indians, some of whom refused to work on their farm plots. Two years earlier, Indian Agent P. P. Wilcox complained of the "indolent nature" of many Apaches who refused to work for the agency farmer appointed to assist in agricultural production. He suggested that "with the aid of an efficient police force under the control of an agency employee in full sympathy with the agent, in his endeavor to compel united action on the part of the Indians, it will be an easy matter to secure greatly increased production during the next year."[42] The agents failed to understand, however, that Apache males believed that farming was women's work and found it very distasteful; consequently, since they had no agricultural work experience, they often became discouraged about farm problems and setbacks that might occur from drought or some other problem.[43]

In February 1887, Captain Pierce, the acting Indian agent, trying to enforce work on a regular and consistent basis, put Mott in charge of a group of Tonto Apaches who were farming along the Gila River less than two miles west of the agency. Mott was assisted by Frank Porter, an agricultural employee who acted as an advisor on farming and irrigation methods. Mott also had the authority to deal with land disputes or any other issues that might arise. Unfortunately, Mott had virtually no experience with Native Americans, and he apparently was authoritarian and somewhat overbearing in his dealings with the Apaches. On duty at San Carlos Agency for less than three months, he apparently became involved in a dispute with Nahdeizaz's father on March 10, 1887. His main complaint seemed to be the old man's lack of enthusiasm in plowing a section along the Gila River. Some years earlier the old Apache had been badly mauled by a grizzly bear and had lost partial use of his right arm, but that did not seem to satisfy either Mott or Porter. Because the Apaches were not coop-erating or meeting work requirements, both men had begun to aggressively order the Apache farmers around. This led to the confrontation with Nahdeizaz.

As members of a Tonto Apache band, Nahdeizaz's family had lived in the mountains near Camp Verde in the north-central part of Arizona, south of Flagstaff; in 1875, they were relocated to San Carlos. In 1884, Indian Agent P. P. Wilcox sent Nahdeizaz with fifty-one other young Apache children to Carlisle Indian School to gain various technical skills, especially in farming.[44] According to one historian, Nahdeizaz was born in 1865; therefore, he would be about twenty-two years of age at the time of the shooting. Historian Dan Thrapp claims that after Nahdeizaz returned to San Carlos in early 1887, some whites at the agency began to call him the Carlisle Kid; this labeling apparently angered him. Nahdeizaz had entered the liminal world; he was neither Indian nor white.

The exact nature of the controversy that led to the shooting is not clear. Thrapp suggests that a land dispute had developed with Nahdeizaz's father, who had been farming a small plot along the Gila River. According to this version of the story, Lieutenant Mott decided that the old man's tract "should be used for some other purpose." When he refused to leave the land, Mott went out to the plot with two scouts and arrested him. This scenario seems improbable, considering the testimony presented at the trial.[45] The real reason for the arrest probably involved the inability of Nahdeizaz's father to properly plow the ground with a horse. With his crippled arm he had difficulty keeping the plow in the ground as the horse pulled; consequently, the plow was being dragged over the ground, to little effect. Lieutenant Mott ordered the arrest and incarceration of the old Apache in the guardhouse.[46] This event immediately provoked a reaction from Nahdeizaz.

After finding out that his father had been locked in the guardhouse, Nahdeizaz grabbed a Colt revolver, mounted his horse, raced after Mott, and confronted him. Nahdeizaz shouted angrily, "What did you put my father in the jail for?" One witness claimed that Mott "asked what he had said." Nahdeizaz retorted, "Now, you want to put me in jail too? You will not put me in jail."[47] Nahdeizaz drew his revolver and fired at Mott. Either the impact knocked the officer off his horse or else he jumped. Mott got to his feet and ran down the hill with Nahdeizaz running behind in hot pursuit, firing as he ran. He also fired at Frank Porter, the farm employee at San Carlos, who quickly retreated from the scene. Nahdeizaz admitted firing "ten shots at the Lieutenant" and inflicting three wounds. One proved fatal.[48]

This murder case typifies the tragedy that sometimes characterized reservation life. After returning from the Carlisle Indian School, Nahdeizaz felt out of place on the reservation, where Apaches eyed him with suspicion. Typically, Native Americans who returned from white schools were accepted by neither whites nor reservation Indians.[49] Given that the conflict involved an inexperienced army officer and a young Apache chafing from white arrogance, such a deadly encounter should not be unexpected. And as will be seen, in a half-day trial, the jury found Nahdeizaz guilty and sentenced him to life imprisonment.[50]

THE PROSECUTION'S CASE

A grand jury of the U.S. District Court, Second Judicial District, County of Maricopa, Arizona Territory indicted Nahdeizaz for murder on May 9, 1887. The indictment specified that the defendant shot Lieutenant Seward Mott with a revolver on the White Mountain Indian Reservation on March 10, 1887. The U.S. attorney also filed a second indictment charging that the defendant "did shoot and wound the said Frank T. Porter" with the intention of killing him.[51] Before the trial began, E. J. Edwards and A. D. Duff, defense counsel, filed a demurrer specifying that the U.S. District Court holding its proceedings in Phoenix, Maricopa County, had no jurisdiction over the defendant. They complained that the crime of murder had been committed on the White Mountain Indian Reservation in Gila County, not in Maricopa County. The reservation was more than 150 miles from Phoenix, whereas it was only thirty-two miles from Globe, the county seat of Gila County. All of the defendant's friends and relatives lived in Gila County as did all of the witnesses supplied by the prosecution. The trial should be held in Gila County, not Maricopa, for the convenience of witnesses, and, of course, this would better serve the ends of justice. The defendant "therefore prays that the Court change the place of trial from this Maricopa County to the County of Gila."[52] The defense filed a second demurrer the following day, claiming that the grand jury "had no legal authority to inquire into the offense charged by reason of its not being within the legal jurisdiction of the County of Maricopa."[53] The judge dismissed the demurrers. On May 11, the trial of Nahdeizaz was held in Phoenix, Maricopa County, under jurisdiction of the Federal District Court with William W. Porter presiding. Owen T. Rouse acted as U.S. district attorney and W. K. Meade, U.S. marshal, served as bailiff. After the jury had been impaneled and sworn by J. E. Walker, and after the reading of the indictment, defense attorneys entered a plea of not guilty.[54]

Beginning with the impaneling of the jury at 10 a.m. on May 11 and finishing with a jury verdict before day's end indicates that this was a remarkably short murder trial even for the nineteenth century, when most criminal cases usually lasted at least two to three days.[55] In cases involving Apache defendants, however, trials seldom lasted more than a day and, of course, this one required only one half of a day. The shortness of the trial can be partially explained by the prosecution and defense counsel; each called only two witnesses to testify. Since this was a case that could have led to a death sentence, this in itself is troubling and indicates that the prosecution and especially the defense counsel failed to ensure that the defendant received a fair trial.

U.S. Prosecutor Owen T. Rouse called Frank T. Porter as his first witness. Porter had been put in charge of directing a group of Apaches farming along the north side of the Gila River. He testified that on April 10, he and Lieutenant Seward Mott were riding over to a farming plot when they were confronted by Nahdeizaz, also riding a horse and armed with a Colt revolver. Rouse asked him what had happened that day before the shooting. Porter testified, "We were going down there—Lieut. Mott and I to show them how to work" in their fields along the

Gila River. Nahdeizaz's father had been plowing with a horse, and Mott had complained "that they were not working very well." Porter noted that the horse apparently did not want to work and "was hauling the plow around on top of the ground."[56] Porter admitted that Lieutenant Mott had ordered the chief of scouts to put "this boy's father in the guard-house." When he and Mott traveled about one or two miles west, they arrived "where an Indian [Kayzay] was planting wheat, or perhaps it was barley." As they were standing there, a man rode up quickly on a horse. Porter noticed that he had a Colt revolver inside his belt. The Apache "jumped off his horse and had his six shooter in his hand and fired one shot at Lieut. Mott." Porter testified that he tried to stop him, and the man "turned around and shot at me; he shot two shots at me when I was on my way to the house."[57] When Nahdeizaz started shooting, Porter, who was unarmed, turned and ran to the Mojave camps to get a revolver. Porter stated that when he returned to the site of the shooting, Nahdeizaz "saw me and started for me on the run with his six shooter. I let him get up to about sixty yards, then I fired at him; he put up both hands and fired at me; then he fired two shots more."[58] Porter found Lieutenant Mott "weak and bleeding a little" in the leg. Porter put Mott on his horse and proceeded to the agency, where Captain Pierce took Mott down and called the army surgeon.

When asked whether Lieutenant Mott was armed, Porter replied, "No, sir; I didn't see any arms about him." Asked about where the victim had been before the shooting, Porter said that both he and Mott were on horseback about fifteen feet away from Nahdeizaz when the shooting began. Asked what the defendant had said to Mott, Porter claimed he heard him say something to the effect that "the Lieutenant was no good."[59] Another source suggested that the "young buck made some surly or threatening remark and the Lieutenant told him to hush up or he might get in the guard house also."[60]

During cross-examination, E. J. Edwards asked Porter if he and Mott had seen the defendant before the fatal encounter. Porter answered, "Yes." He remembered that Mott had complained that "the Indians [were] not putting the plow in the ground."[61] Porter, however, claimed that Mott did not speak to the defendant directly when they saw him immediately before the shooting. The witness also admitted that Mott had put the defendant's father in the guardhouse on the day of the shooting. Porter stated that he first saw the defendant near where the lieutenant had ordered his father put in jail. Asked about the physical abilities of Nahdeizaz's father, Porter replied that "a bear had bit his arm" and he found it difficult to do hard physical labor. During the cross-examination Porter repeated that, during the shooting, he had heard Nahdeizaz say that "Mott was no good." Nahdeizaz said some other words, but Porter could not remember what they were. Porter testified that it was about "one-half or three-quarters of an hour" after the defendant's father had been put in the guardhouse when Nahdeizaz commenced shooting. There was one other Apache about "forty yards" from the shooting.[62] Defense counsel Edwards asked Porter how long Lieutenant Mott had been at San Carlos. Despite objections by the prosecution, the judge allowed him to answer the question. Porter answered, "I think he had been there two months."[63] The witness claimed that he had been hired as a farmer to help teach the Apaches better agricultural techniques. Porter admitted that Mott had acted as a superintendent in charge of a group of Indians and had the power to enforce all rules on the reservation. Captain Pierce, however, functioned as the head of the agency and had assigned several officers to work with and supervise groups of Apaches on the reservation. Porter admitted that he was excited at the time of the shooting; nevertheless, he was satisfied that the defendant was the person who killed Mott.

During redirect testimony by U.S. Prosecutor Rouse, Porter

stated that the place where the defendant had been farming was about two miles west of the agency and located on the north side of the Gila River. Asked about the exact location, Porter stated that the Gila River "makes a bend right there; it might be a hundred yards."[64] The witness insisted that both he and Mott were unarmed at the time of the shooting. He testified that when Nahdeizaz fired his first shot, Lieutenant Mott was on his horse. He fired three times from the horse. Then Mott jumped off his horse and began running and ended up about one hundred yards from the original spot of the shooting. Asked how close together the first three shots were, he replied, "About as fast as a man would shoot."[65] This would, of course, suggest heat of passion, not deliberate malice aforethought.

U.S. Prosecutor Rouse next called Dr. T. B. Davis, San Carlos army surgeon, to the stand. Davis testified that he had breakfast with Mott at about 8 a.m. on March 10, the day of the shooting. When he saw Mott again at about 10:30 a.m., he was still in good condition. The next time he saw him, however, he was "suffering from several gun-shot wounds."[66] He had three gunshot wounds, "one in the arm, one in the thigh, and the third in the buttock, penetrating the pelvic cavity." Davis testified that "the first wound I think was given while he was mounted." The first and second wounds were just "flesh wounds"; however, "the third wound entered the pelvic cavity; it passed transversely directly across, cutting the bladder in its passage."[67] The third wound proved to be fatal; Davis last saw Lieutenant Mott alive at around 8:30 a.m. on March 11, the day after the shooting. Mott died at about 2 p.m. on March 11.

Asked about the location of the farm, the doctor stated that the agency building was about two miles from where the shooting had taken place. Questioned whether he knew the defendant, Davis claimed that he had seen the defendant many times; Nahdeizaz and other Apache farmers passed the army quarters every day on their way to their farms. They had been working for some time on a new ditch to irrigate their farm plots.[68]

THE DEFENSE'S CASE

Similar to other trials involving Apache defendants, during his testimony "the defendant was examined through two inter- preters: Mr. Henry Garfías interpreting from English to Spanish, and Mr. Antonio Díaz interpreting from Spanish to Indian [Apache]."[69] Questioned about the shooting, Nahdeizaz claimed that it all started after Lieutenant Mott "put his cap- tain in the guard-house." The following morning, Nahdeizaz went after his horses in order to begin plowing. His father had been helping on the farm; however, he could only "work with one hand."[70] After he had started plowing, the chief of scouts "came over and put his father in the guard-house." Nahdeizaz testified that Lieutenant Mott "told him [his father] to take this note to the Agency or he would be locked up."[71] Apparently, the father failed to give the agent the note, but soon the scouts came over to talk to his father. When Nahdeizaz saw that the scouts were taking him to the guardhouse, he jumped on his horse and overtook Lieutenant Mott, who was sitting on his horse talking with "some Indians plowing close by."[72] (This tes- timony indicates the difficulty in understanding the translation of the two interpreters. Nahdeizaz would not have used the word *Indian* to describe Apache farmers. He would most likely have said Tonto Apache or Apache.) Nahdeizaz admitted that he spoke to the lieutenant "in an angry manner" when he asked the officer why he had put his father in jail. What actually hap- pened during this confrontation is unclear. The two interpreters may have made mistakes at this point as to who said what.

The testimony suggests that Mott must have threatened to put Nahdeizaz in jail with his father. It is possible that Mott did not understand what the defendant had said to him in the angry

exchange. Apparently Mott asked him what he had said; however, the interpreters failed to state what the defendant had said
in reply. Nahdeizaz said to Lieutenant Mott, "Now, you want
to put me in jail too?" and further exclaimed, "You will not put
me in jail." This testimony reveals that Mott had, indeed,
threatened to arrest him at this time; otherwise, why would the
defendant have responded that way? Almost immediately,
Nahdeizaz fired at Lieutenant Mott. After the first shot, Porter
came toward the defendant, but after he fired one shot at
Porter, Porter turned and ran. Defense counsel asked Nahdeizaz
how long Mott "had been there overseeing the Indians?" Prosecutor Rouse objected but was overruled. Nahdeizaz answered,
"He was there a short while."[73] Rouse asked Nahdeizaz how
many shots he had fired. Nahdeizaz replied that he had "fired
ten shots at the Lieutenant." Questioned on what Mott was
doing during the shooting, the defendant replied that Mott
"was in a dead run and he was running after him."[74] Nahdeizaz
testified that Mott had been sitting on his horse "looking at
him" when he first fired at him.

By placing Nahdeizaz on the stand to testify on his own
behalf, defense counsel E. J. Edwards had taken a calculated
risk, but one that was used often by inexperienced, court-
appointed attorneys representing Native Americans. By doing
this, he opened up his client to cross-examination by the prosecutor, which proved to be crucial in reaching the final verdict.
Nahdeizaz's testimony tended to counter the possibility of a
heated and angry outburst because he had chased Mott down
the hill, reloaded his gun, and continued to fire at his victim.
The chance of the jury accepting mitigating factors concerning
heat of passion virtually vanished along with any chance of a
reduced charge of second degree murder. It proved to be a
costly defense tactic.

Defense counsel called Kayzay, an Apache farmer, as a witness on behalf of the defendant. This witness was also exam-

ined through the two interpreters, Garfías and Díaz. Asked whether he had seen the shooting, Kayzay said, "Yes, sir; I was present when the shots were fired."[75] Apparently, he was about five yards away when the confrontation occurred, yet he claimed that he did not "hear any words between them." Asked to show what the distance was, he pointed to some men sitting nearby and said that was the distance, about fifteen feet. Mott was sitting on his horse, which was sideways to the defendant and looking right at Nahdeizaz before the shooting. After the defendant fired the first shot, the lieutenant "jumped off [the horse] and ran afoot." Mott, with Nahdeizaz in pursuit, quickly disappeared over a hill, "but he could hear the shooting."[76] The witness had been plowing in his field when the shooting took place on his farm. He testified that he saw the defendant fire at least five shots at Mott.

As suggested previously, this was a very short trial, about a half-day experience, and defense counsel failed to call a single character witness that might have shown some mitigating factors in favor of the defendant. The introduction of testimony by friends, family members, and possibly San Carlos Agency employees might have been useful in showing that Nahdeizaz's years at Carlisle had been a disaster and, since returning, he had become somewhat alienated by this experience. For example, he had been called the Carlisle Kid, a name that he did not appreciate, especially if he had had any trouble during his years attending the Indian school, as most young Apache men did. And here he was, trying to use his skills learned at Carlisle, and this young "shave tail" officer, with no experience with Apaches, was threatening him with jail time for being "insolent." Defense counsel could have pushed the "heat of passion" factor because the shots came so fast and in quick succession after the short argument between Mott and Nahdeizaz. By opening his client to cross-examination that revealed ten shots had been fired, any chance at mitigating factors virtually disappeared. Federal law recognized only murder in the first degree, consequently, the defense attorneys faced a very difficult task in defending their client. This is, unfortunately, typical of court-appointed attorneys who had little knowledge of criminal law or how to effectively try a murder case.

THE VERDICT

The testimony was closed, and the prosecutor and defense counsel concluded their arguments to the jury. At this point, Judge William W. Porter gave his instructions to the jury. He explained that Nahdeizaz had been indicted for killing with malice aforethought Lieutenant Seward Mott on March 10, 1887, at San Carlos on the White Mountain Indian Reservation. Judge Porter said, "The jury is left to determine the degree of the crime from the evidence before them." The legal test for murder, "Is the killing willful, deliberate, and premeditated?" The judge continued: if the jury believes that the "wounds were inflicted with malice aforethought, then they should find the defendant guilty of murder unless the Jury find that at the time of the shooting by defendant that he was in danger of his own life."[77] Finally, "Every person or persons convicted of murder of the first degree shall suffer death if the jury affix the penalty of death in their verdict; and if the jury do not affix the penalty of death in their verdict, every person or persons convicted of murder of the first degree shall suffer imprisonment in the Territorial Prison for life."[78] After retiring briefly to deliberate, the jury returned with the verdict. "We, the Jury, duly empaneled and sworn in the above entitle action, do, upon our oaths, find: the defendant guilty of murder in the first degree. M. H. Sherman, Foreman."[79] The jury did not affix the death penalty; consequently, the defendant was sentenced to life in prison. How long the jury deliberated is unknown; however, considering that it was a half-day trial, it could not have been more than an hour or two. Judge

Porter sentenced Nahdeizaz to life to be served in the Yuma Territorial Prison. Since he was a federal prisoner, after spending a few
months at Yuma, U.S. marshals took custody and transported
him to the state prison at Menard, Illinois, which handled federal
prisoners on a contractual basis. What Nahdeizaz's experience
was like at Menard is unknown. In 1889, however, his case,
along with eight other Apache cases, were linked to the Gonshayee and Captain Jack cases on appeal to the U.S. Supreme
Court. He was released in 1889 and returned to San Carlos
Agency to await disposition of his case in the Gila County criminal courts.

NAHDEIZAZ'S SECOND TRIAL

After U.S. marshals returned Nahdeizaz to San Carlos, Lieutenant F. B. Fowler pressed charges against him, and J. D.
McCabe, district attorney of Gila County, secured an indictment for murder on October 23, 1889.[80] Fowler was the officer
who had accompanied the remains of Lieutenant Seward Mott
on their return to his family in Utica, New York. He had been a
fellow officer and one of Mott's friends at San Carlos.

Nahdeizaz's second trial occurred on October 25, 1889, in
Globe, Arizona, with Judge Joseph H. Kibbey, Arizona Territorial Court in Gila County, presiding. J. D. McCabe represented
the territory, and Mills Van Wagenen acted as court-appointed
defense counsel.[81] There are no surviving preliminary hearings
or trial transcripts of the testimony presented in this second
trial. The defendant pled not guilty. The jury was impaneled,
testimony taken, argument by counsel, deliberation by the jury,
and the defendant found guilty in a one-day trial. At his second
trial, the defendant was the only defense witness and, according
to historian Jess G. Hayes, Nahdeizaz "faced a courtroom
packed with hostile—or, at best, indifferent—spectators, an
unsympathetic judge, and a self-assured prosecutor."[82] Hayes

claims that defense counsel "Van Wagenen made an eloquent plea for mercy but the result was never in doubt."[83] Four days later, Judge Kibbey sentenced Nahdeizaz to death, and the execution date was set for December 27, 1889, to take place in the Gila County jail yard in Globe, Arizona. Nahdeizaz's trial took place at the same time that Apache Kid and four other scouts were being retried for either murder or attempted murder. All of these trials were completed in just two days. While discussing the trials of Nahdeizaz and seven other Apaches charged with murder in Globe, Arizona, Edward Arhelger, an observer of the brief legal proceedings, stated, "All were promptly found guilty, which I think myself was wrong, but the sentiment was such that a good Indian was a dead Indian."[84]

FINAL OBSERVATIONS

Returning to the killings committed by the two Carlisle graduates, there are some similarities as well as differences between them. For example, both of their victims, lieutenants Edward W. Casey and Seward Mott, were in command of Indian scouts before their deaths. Casey, however, had considerable military experience whereas Mott had recently graduated from West Point, and his tour of duty at San Carlos Agency, unfortunately, proved to be his first and last military assignment. Though Mott was receiving his first taste of Native American culture, Casey had an extensive background dealing with Cheyenne and Sioux warriors and understood many of their social habits. With his vast experience, Casey "was widely regarded as a prospective general."[85] Casey had served as an assistant instructor of tactics at West Point from 1880 to 1884, and possibly had instructed Mott, who was still attending the military academy at that time. Finally, both men were killed by Carlisle graduates who were experiencing considerable difficulty readjusting to reservation life.

Intriguing parallels also exist between the accused Nah-deizaz and Plenty Horses: both had attended Carlisle Indian School at about the same time and may have been acquaintances. Nahdeizaz arrived in 1884, one year after Plenty Horses began his educational experience. It is very likely that these two young men knew each other and may have become friends while taking classes on agriculture practices at school. They were forced to attend Carlisle, where they were not allowed to speak their native languages and had their hair cut off and their native garb destroyed. This series of events must have created increased anxiety and psychological trauma for both young men, who suffered from culture shock. Born in 1869, Plenty Horses arrived at Carlisle at age fourteen and returned to the reservation five years later prepared to make a new start. Like many other "returned students," Plenty Horses, after going back to the Rosebud Reservation in Dakota Territory, encountered great difficulty trying to use his newly acquired skills. During the grand jury hearing, Plenty Horses eloquently explained his reasoning for killing Casey.

> I am an Indian. Five years I attended Carlisle and was educated in the ways of the white man. When I returned to my people, I was an outcast among them. I was no longer an Indian. I was not a white man. I was lonely. I shot the lieutenant so I might make a place for myself among my people. Now I am one of them. I shall be hung and the Indians will bury me as a warrior. They will be proud of me. I am satisfied.[86]

When the second trial of Plenty Horses reached the court-room, defense counsel claimed that the killing had occurred during a war. The U.S. Army suddenly became aware that if it refused to support this claim, the officers and men of the U.S. 7th Cavalry could also be tried for the murder of some 180 or more members of Big Foot's band of Sioux killed at Wounded

Knee. Consequently, General Nelson Miles ordered Captain Frank D. Baldwin to testify in court that the killing occurred during a time of war.[87] Although the murder charges against Plenty Horses were dismissed, historian Robert Utley relates that he did not gain his wish to be hanged as a warrior; instead, he lived in a "one-room log cabin on Oak Creek, 'quite unloved' by neighbors and acquaintances."[88] Plenty Horses died on June 15, 1933, on the Rosebud Reservation.

Like Asa Daklugie, Jason Betzinez, Tolma, Stagon, Robert McIntosh, and many other Apache men, Nahdeizaz suffered from culture shock and found it difficult to adjust to conditions upon returning to the San Carlos Agency. As with Plenty Horses, local Apache and white leaders on the reservation did not accept him. Nahdeizaz suffered great anguish while living in a liminal world betwixt and between two cultural groups. Finally, being called the Carlisle Kid and bossed around by white farmers and army officers apparently pushed him to the edge. In an audacious display of anger and uncontrollable rage, he confronted and killed Lieutenant Mott, the most visible symbol of his oppressed existence. Sadly, there were many other examples of broken lives throughout the American West; cultural destruction meant disaster for Native Americans in the nineteenth century.

CHAPTER 4

BATDISH

Red Man, White Justice

The scouts all said it was Massai did the killing.

AL SIEBER

ON SATURDAY, JULY 12, 1890, young Edward Baker got up, had his breakfast, and then walked about 220 yards south of the house through the potato patch and began to cut down a cottonwood tree. As he began chopping the tree, apparently two Apaches approached him from the south. They were presumed to be Apaches because they left moccasin tracks. After they crossed a fence, one of them took a position behind a poplar tree, where he crouched down and aimed a rifle at Baker. He quickly fired a shot into his back, mortally wounding him. The assailant then approached the victim, picked up an axe, and whacked Baker in the neck two or three times, almost severing the head. Then the killer walked north up to the house while his partner turned east, passed the strawberry patch, took Baker's horse, and then walked over to the house to join the murderer. The two Apaches entered and ransacked the house, throwing blankets, provisions, a teapot, two guns without ammunition, a sack of flour, a coat, pants, and other items out the door and onto the porch and the ground on the south side of the building.[1]

This killing occurred in an isolated region in the middle of the Sierra Ancha Mountains, far from any town or village in Gila County, Arizona Territory. Robert S. Knowles, the nearest neighbor, had a homestead about a mile away, and three miles farther east there was a series of small ranches that were scattered south along Cherry Creek to the Salt River. Baker's place was located at an elevation of about seventy-five hundred feet, near the summit of what became known as Baker's Mountain. The crime scene was situated about five miles west of Fort Apache and San Carlos reservations and about twelve miles north of the Salt River. Globe, the nearest city and county seat of Gila County, was approximately thirty miles south of Baker's Mountain. On Monday, July 14, Edward Ingalls, a neighbor, visited the farmer's homestead and found Baker lying face down, dead. He immediately went to the ranch of Baker's father and informed him that his son had been murdered. By this time, because of the heat, the body "was somewhat bloated, and smelt bad."[2] George Shute and Wallace Kenton Hinton, neighboring ranchers, and J. H. Baker, the victim's father, soon arrived at the crime scene; they quickly buried the badly decomposing body. After examining the crime scene, they discovered tracks leading from the body to the house. There were two sets of tracks near the trail leading up to Baker's place, and one set of footprints led to the house from the body. George Shute found evidence that someone had "sat down behind" a poplar tree and shot from that point. Shute admitted that he and many other ranchers had been tracking around the site so much that he "couldn't discern whether it was our tracks or moccasin tracks" of the killers.[3] This trampling of the crime scene complicated the process of locating and following the trail. About two days later, Al Sieber arrived to track the killers. This rugged country created great difficulty for Sieber and his

Apache scouts, who were sent from the San Carlos Agency to examine and investigate the crime scene, track, and, hopefully, locate the killers. Despite changes in homicide investigation that had been developed and used in London and Paris, and in New York and Philadelphia at the end of the nineteenth century, Sieber and his scouts, working in a primitive environment on the frontier, were still saddled with crude methods in searching for and collecting evidence at crime scenes that would enable them to solve the murder and find the killers.

HOMICIDE INVESTIGATION

Scientific crime detection first gained support in London and Paris during the early part of the nineteenth century. In 1842, the discovery of a decapitated and limbless body of a woman and the escape of the suspect, Daniel Good, in London, alarmed many citizens. Eventually the legal authorities captured, tried, convicted, and executed Good. This terrible crime and sensational trial pressured authorities to establish a detective force to investigate and solve homicides and other major crimes. Within a year, twelve police detectives became headquartered at Scotland Yard and embarked on a new era of scientific criminal investigation. Although Scotland Yard grew rather slowly, it soon gained the confidence of the public and by the 1870s had developed a reputation for solving homicides.

One of the most important aids in investigating and solving crimes was the development of the science of fingerprinting. This new method was first introduced in 1858 by William Herschel, an English criminologist; however, at the turn of the century, a major breakthrough occurred when Edward Henry, Scotland Yard, devised a method of scientifically classifying fingerprints into categories that could be searched through fingerprint files collected from criminals to identify the guilty party. Fingerprints quickly became the preferred method of criminal identification, and in 1903, Scotland Yard authorities proved its value by identifying 3,642 out of 11,919 fingerprint searches completed that year.[4] Mark Twain developed an insightful and prophetic fictional account about fingerprinting when he published a story in 1883 that included the identification of a murderer through the use of a thumb print discovered at the crime scene. Eleven years later, he used fictitious fingerprint identification in a courtroom scene in his novel *Pudd'nhead Wilson*. In this dramatic scene, Twain's character Pudd'nhead produced a bloody handprint taken from a murder scene as evidence, along with the handprint of the killer. Pudd'nhead claimed that every person has these distinguishing lines or prints on their hands and feet. They are "his signature, his physiological autograph, so to speak, and his autograph cannot be counterfeited."[5] The lawyer then produced the handprints of the guilty party and solved the murder. In this popular 1894 novel, Twain cleverly exploited the newly developed science of identification that was being widely used in Great Britain.

Similarly, Sir Arthur Conan Doyle's Sherlock Holmes detective stories popularized the concept of forensic science during the 1880s and provided a renewed interest in scientific crime detection. A trained physician, Doyle added a new dimension to detective stories by introducing scientific deduction and forensic science as a means of catching criminals. Forensic science refers to the method of analyzing physical evidence that is to be presented to a court of law in a criminal case. The main purpose of forensic science is to identify evidence at the crime scene, compare it with other samples that may have been left by the criminal, reconstruct the crime based upon these various pieces of evidence, and then transform this information into an acceptable format to be used in court. Such scientific detection at a crime scene could include searching for weapons, footprints, fingerprints, articles of clothing, blood, hair, and a variety of other pieces of evidence left by the victim and the perpetrator.

Forensic scientists believe that every criminal leaves something at a crime scene and that this information can be used for positive identification. The process included collecting and preserving the evidence, taking photographs, casting plaster impressions of footprints, and other scientific examinations of the crime scene. Finally, analysis would be conducted on the evidence in order to provide exhibits that would enable the district attorney to prosecute the accused.

By midnineteenth century, the use of chemistry and microscopes in solving homicides had become a well-established technique in major cities in Great Britain, France, and the United States. Dr. Alfred Swaine Taylor, a British physician, published a series of groundbreaking books on forensic sciences, and his *Principles and Practices of Medical Jurisprudence* (1865) set the standard for decades both in European countries and in America. Medical schools worldwide used his books on forensic science in their classes on medical jurisprudence. Taylor held a professorship in medical jurisprudence for over forty years at Guy's Hospital Medical School in London. Although he specialized in toxicology (there were many poisoning homicides in Europe), his books included extensive discussions on head wounds, the determining of cause and time of death, and a variety of other subjects to aid criminal investigation.[6]

In an 1876 essay on scientific crime detection in *Appletons' Journal*, Dr. Allan McL. Hamilton discussed the collection of criminal evidence and noted that detectives were able "to preserve an exact mold of the footprint" found at a crime scene by using plaster of Paris, a method commonly employed by police investigators in the nineteenth century.[7] Unfortunately, no impressions, photographs, or measurements were made of the footprints found at the Baker crime scene in the Sierra Ancha Mountains to compare with the feet of the accused. From a modern-day perspective, this would seem to be the most basic procedure to follow at a homicide crime scene. By using the

foot measurement systems developed by French scientist
Alphonse Bertillon, a nineteenth-century crime investigator
could examine bare footprints and develop a profile of the
height and weight of the criminal who left them.[8] In 1892, Scotland Yard issued orders to use a new footprint impression technique that included a mixture of paraffin wax and resin, a sub-
stance found to be superior to plaster of Paris.[9] If a cast was not
taken, the investigators could still take photographs and use a
ruler to measure the length and width of the footprints and
determine their direction and destination.

Although it is unlikely that such forensic techniques would
have been used at San Carlos in the late nineteenth century, the
use of footprint impressions could have had an important
impact on the case of Baker's murder if they had been measured
and preserved. Despite various attempts during the nineteenth
century to discredit footprints, courts customarily accepted
them as admissible and credible evidence. For example, in
People v. McCurdy, a California murder case appealed in 1886,
defense counsel claimed that the original court had erred in
accepting footprints as evidence. The California Supreme
Court, however, upheld the guilty verdict, ruling that the witness "measured the foot-prints found at that point, which cor-
responded with similar marks found in the vicinity of the body
of the deceased . . . and by him measured and found to fit the
boots of defendant."[10] In an appeal of a robbery case that
hinged on circumstantial evidence, the California Supreme
Court also upheld footprint evidence that tied the defendant to
the crime scene: "The prosecution gave evidence that certain
boot-marks of peculiar characteristics were found the day after
the robbery at the place, and were traced . . . into a corral at
the place of residence of defendant Myers."[11] The court held
that footprint evidence was admissible. As examples such as
these document, California case law reveals that footprints
often played an important role when introduced as evidence in

murder or robbery trials. In Arizona Territory, such methods were not commonly employed in criminal investigations; however, there were law enforcement authorities at the San Carlos Agency, especially the Apache scouts, ready to investigate homicides committed in remote regions.

APACHE SCOUTS

In 1871, General George Crook arrived in Arizona to enforce control over the Apaches. After holding talks with Coyotero Apaches at San Carlos, he was able to recruit many of

White Mountain Apache Scouts, 1885. They tracked criminals and served at the San Carlos Guardhouse.
Courtesy Arizona State Library, Archives and Public Records, Phoenix, No. 98-6108.

them to serve as scouts. He quickly organized a company of
Apache scouts under the command of Captain Guy V. Henry.
Crook understood the importance of using Apache scouts in
campaigns against various Apache tribes. By offering them
employment, horses, weapons, and other inducements, he was
able to convince them that it would be to their advantage to
cooperate in waging war with the Chiricahuas and other tribes
who had been their own enemies for decades. He began to conduct destructive raids against various Apache bands throughout
central Arizona, quickly bringing them in line and forcing them
to relocate to San Carlos. When Crook encountered problems
with Apaches who had left San Carlos on raids, he ordered the
Apache scouts to capture or kill the leaders. When several were
brought in, they "begged to be allowed to remain" at San
Carlos. Crook "finally compromised by letting them stay, provided they would bring in the heads of certain of the chiefs who
were ringleaders, which they agreed to do. A couple of morn-
ings afterwards they brought in seven heads."[12] The Apache
scouts were relentless and proved to be ruthless with any "renegade" Apaches who resisted them. After one scout had been
killed in a fire fight, "another expedition went out to the scene
of the fight . . . came up on the Indian camp, and killed the
whole party, regardless of age or sex." They could be unfor-
giving.[13]

Captain John G. Bourke, who served under General Crook
during the early campaigns against the Apaches in 1872–1873,
kept a diary that detailed troop movements and the use of
scouts. On December 9, 1872, he noted that "Eskiminzin
promised to aid in the extermination of hostile Apaches." They
enlisted thirty-one Apache scouts.[14] About a week later they
received "a dispatch from Archie MacIntosh stating that the
advance guard had found a ranchería of Indians and had
exchanged shots."[15] Their uncanny ability to track and find the

enemy always impressed Bourke. Two weeks later, ninety-eight Pima Indian scouts helped his unit surprise the enemy, and they killed twenty-five "hostiles" near Tonto Creek. On January 23, 1873, Bourke recorded that twenty-six new scouting recruits were selected for Crook's army. Most of the units had more than forty-six scouts serving with them.[16] Despite heavy rainfall, which made tracking difficult, the scouts quickly picked up the trail that led to Black Mesa. With the aid of the scouts, Crook's army traveled over twelve hundred miles, killed five hundred "hostile" Indians, and forced the rest to surrender and go to San Carlos.[17]

Lieutenant Colonel W. H. Carter quickly learned that when Apache scouts were used against other Apache tribes perceived as enemies, the scouts operated "with the unerring instincts of the bloodhound, and . . . killed them as remorselessly as they would have done their white enemies." Some officers, however, realized that the "Indian scouts knew the terrain, possessed greater experience in fighting Indians," thus they provided "many practical advantages for army troops."[18] Colonel O. L. Hein observed that the Apache scouts "proved to be of invaluable assistance, as they were acquainted with the location of the haunts of the hostiles, and were familiar with their mode of warfare."[19] General Crook was so interested in his Apache scouts that he "preferred the scouts' company to that of his own officers." This irritated Lieutenant Colonel Richard Irving Dodge, one of his officers, who complained that Crook "scarcely treats [Ranald] McKenzie and I decently, but he will spend hours chatting pleasantly with an Indian or a dirty scout."[20] Captain Bourke displayed a similar interest in Apaches, noting that "nearly all the talk I had with anybody was with" the Apache scouts.[21] Bourke virtually lived with the Apache scouts when they were on the move. Bourke had praise especially for Alchesay, Chiquito, and Nantaje. He claimed that "the longer we knew the Apache scouts, the better we liked them."[22]

After subduing the Apaches in March 1875, Crook received orders to serve in the Great Plains war against the Lakota and Cheyenne, but he returned to command the Department of Arizona on September 4, 1882. Crook soon realized that Geronimo and other "renegade" Apaches had left the reservation and were raiding all over southeast Arizona and had to be punished and returned to San Carlos. Once again he recruited Apache scouts and hired Al Sieber as a major guide and chief of scouts. Hunting down Geronimo proved to be a challenge that required a large number of scouts. Crook placed Captain Emmet Crawford in control of 193 Apache scouts, while Lieutenant Charles B. Gatewood commanded 100 scouts and Captain Wirt Davis, a similar number. Despite eventually tracking down, meeting with, and gaining Geronimo's promise to return to San Carlos, Crook could not keep the "renegade" from taking off into Mexico again. Crook had proved that Apache scouts were essential if you wanted to hunt down and capture Apaches who left the reservation. Geronimo's final raid forced Crook's hand; he resigned and left Arizona.[23]

After assuming control of the Department of Arizona, General Nelson Miles, who did not trust the Apache scouts, dismissed all of them. He chose to use regular troops during his hunt for Geronimo. His campaign against the Apaches proved to be fruitless and finally forced Miles to reinstate some of the scouts, who were sent to find and talk with Geronimo. It was a successful maneuver when Captain Gatewood, accompanied by Kayitah and Martine, two Apache scouts, found Geronimo's stronghold in Mexico. Despite this brief hiatus, the Apache scouts continued in service throughout the nineteenth century. The San Carlos Agency listed thirty scouts attached to the agency in July 19, 1892. They were led by Acting First Sergeant

Goodygooday, who had served in Clum's San Carlos Police in the 1870s. There were two other sergeants and two corporals, and the rest were privates.[24] The San Carlos Apache scouts proved their ability, especially in the art of tracking the enemy during wartime and, of course, during peacetime, when they apprehended suspected criminals.

Scout Tracking Skills

The Apaches were natural scouts who had learned the art of tracking game animals such as deer in the deserts of Arizona Territory from an early age. Over a period of ten to fifteen years they honed the people-tracking skills that would make them famous and assure the U.S. Army that they were safe behind the advance party of Apache scouts who acted as a screen for the cavalry. While serving in the Pershing campaign in Mexico, 1916–1917, Lieutenant H. B. Wharfield formed some negative first impressions working with Apache scouts. He had a rather low opinion of them, especially when he first saw "twenty short, stocky, pleasant mannered individuals" who averaged about five feet, six inches and some who were overweight.[25] Wharfield, however, quickly learned the true value of the Apache scouts and concluded, "From what I have learned about the Indians myself I have not the slightest doubt that if they had been put on the trail they would have been able to follow it to the end." In Mexico he observed their trailing skills while hunting deer. Wharfield noted that "the Apaches trailed and found their game so quietly and with so little sign of doing anything unusual."[26] Through discussions with the scouts he learned that when they found the trail, they began to hunt by understanding the habits of the deer and did not have to follow the trail closely.

The Apache scouts acted as an advance guard during troop movements and Wharfield observed that the Apache's extreme caution was "one of the qualities that makes him a perfect scout. It would be almost impossible to surprise an outfit that had a detachment of Apache scouts in its front."[27] Initially, the lieutenant thought that their trailing methods were of the hit-or-miss category, but after watching them for a while he observed, "I am willing to state I believe trailing is a science with the Apaches. . . . Show them a trail and they will take you to the person or thing that made the trail."[28] Once, while searching for U.S. Army deserters in Mexico, he observed what he considered to be one of the most convincing examples of their trailing skills. The scouts "started south along a trail which followed a narrow river bed. The trail crossed the river about fifty times in half as many miles. About ten miles from camp the scouts, who were always watching the ground, saw the tracks of an American horse going south, and soon they announced that there was a Mexican mule with this horse." They concluded that they were following an American deserter who was being accompanied by a Mexican showing him the way south. After following them for miles, "they lost the trail completely for perhaps fifteen minutes. They circled out widely and finally one man whistled and waved his arm,"—he had found the trail.[29] After another example of the scouts trailing other deserters, Wharfield stated, "Any lingering doubts I may have had as to their ability, were entirely dispelled by this exhibition." After trailing a party of deserters south, one of the officers accompanying Wharfield and the scouts used his field glasses to locate what he believed to be their camp south of them. Sergeant Chicken pointed in the other direction and said, "No, they gone north." After moving north for about one or two hours, they came across the deserters. This example of tracking convinced Wharfield "of their absolute reliability as trailers."[30] Captain John Bourke believed that Apache scouts had animal-like virtues such as "vision as keen as a hawk's" and had a "tread as untiring and as stealthy as the panther's."[31]

During the Pershing campaign into Mexico, Lieutenant James A. Shannon commanded the unit and had only one bad experience with the scouts. About three hundred miles below the border, they obtained liquor and became drunk and quarrelsome. "Shannon lectured the scouts" and experienced no problems after this episode.[32] The scouts proved to be effective in tracking Pancho Villa's men, who were cutting the Signal Corps telegraph lines. When assigned to track down the culprits, "upon locating a cut, the Apaches picked up the trail that was not discernible to the other soldiers since there was no obvious horse or human tracks. They followed the 'invisible trail' for twelve miles without wavering in any direction, until they came upon" their quarry. As Pershing's raid began to wane, "the Apaches spent a significant amount of their remaining seven months of Mexican service tracking down American deserters." They quickly "located the 'invisible trail' based on the mere evidence that a fast moving horse had stumbled in a prairie dog hole and a piece of cactus had been broken off." They captured their deserter within twenty-four hours of picking up the trail.[33]

The tradition of using Apache scouts for tracking criminals and deserters in Arizona continued well into the twentieth century before the U.S. Army phased them out. Company A of the Apache scouts originally stationed at Fort Apache, Arizona, were reassigned to Fort Huachuca. These twenty veteran scouts, who had served with Pershing already, had familiarity with the Sonoran Desert and the Sierra Madre range that had been a frequent haunt for Chiricahua Apaches during the nineteenth century. Askeldelinay and Deklay, who had been serving as scouts since 1879, had participated in the Geronimo campaign in 1886. Sometime later, Lieutenant Wharfield, who commanded these scouts reassigned to Fort Huachuca, still "marveled at the Apaches' tracking ability and their willingness to suffer extreme privation in achieving a goal." They proved to be well suited "for tracking the remote terrain of Arizona's southern borders" and often were used to locate "lost tourists and AWOL soldiers."[34]

TRACKING THE KILLERS

After discovering the body of Edward Baker, the local authorities sent a telegram to the Indian agent at the San Carlos Agency requesting that he send Apache scouts to track the killers. On Wednesday, July 16, Al Sieber and several scouts arrived at the crime scene from San Carlos, a twenty-four-hour journey. After examining the area around where the body had been lying (they had already buried it), Sieber complained that the crime scene had been badly "trampled" by people walking around. After a methodical inspection of the crime scene, Sieber's scouts found three tracks but could not determine if two or three people had made them. Less than a mile from Baker's ranch, they found items left by the killers, including .45- and .44-caliber bullets, flour, and coffee, which had been taken from the ranch. Sieber and his company of scouts trailed the killers to Robert Knowles's ranch, about one mile east of the crime scene. The scouts followed the trail right up to the house, which had been entered. The killers had broken open a trunk, and about four hundred yards farther along the trail, the scouts found some of Knowles's papers and photographs that had been thrown away. The Apache scouts discovered two sets of moccasin prints and trailed them past Knowles' where they split off in a different direction.[35] It rained, and the scouts could not find the two moccasin trails the next day, but it took only about three hours to find the horse tracks, which they followed south down Cherry Creek to within six miles of S. S. Patterson's ranch. At that point they found some bullet molds. On

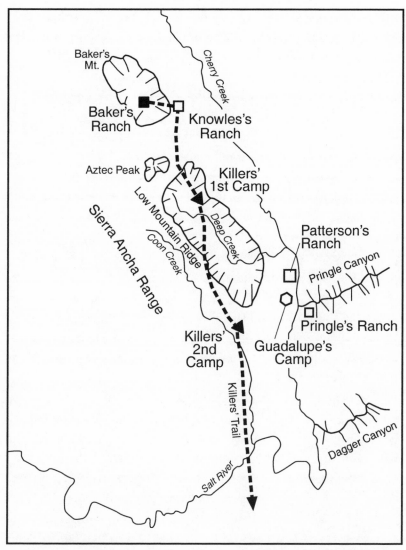

Map showing the trail followed by the Apache scouts tracking Baker's killers, 1890. *Courtesy of Melodie Tune, graphic artist, Instructional Technology Services, San Diego State University.*

July 17, Sieber and his scouts found a "squaw" who had been shot and a "girl taken away from her," but they lost the trail again at Coon Creek. It required six hours for three scouts to follow the killer "three or four miles, until he struck Coon Creek; he kept in the water all the way; that is where we lost it."[36] On July 18, Patterson and Sheriff Thompson arrived at the scouts' camp and informed Sieber that some Apaches had been camped near Patterson's place.

Despite being able to discover and follow the trail from the crime scene south to the Salt River and beyond to Wheatfields and then to Black Mountain, Sieber and the Apache scouts were unable to find and apprehend any of the killers. Considering the effects of inclement weather, the lateness of reaching the crime scene, and the obvious attempts by the killers to throw off any trackers by entering and riding down Coon Creek, it should not be surprising that the scouts were unable to find them. Nevertheless, Sieber and his men demonstrated once again the skills of Apache scouts in tracking criminals in Arizona Territory.

According to J. D. McCabe, the Gila County prosecutor, Batdish, Natsin, Guadalupe, and Bakelcle had been camped on Cherry Creek near Patterson's ranch on the day of the killing. Patterson testified that several of the men left the camp, traveled west up into the Sierra Ancha Mountains, and returned late in the day with two deer that they had shot. After bringing back the deer, they immediately packed up and headed north along Cherry Creek and eventually turned northeast to Cibicue, located on Fort Apache Reservation. There were seven in Guadalupe's camp, Natsin, Batdish, and "the other boy," two women, and a girl. After spending about seven days in Cibicue, Guadalupe, an Apache scout, traveled "to Camp Apache to draw his pay." Guadalupe was arrested by Mickey Free and several other scouts and brought before Lieutenant Jones at

Camp Apache, where the sheriff informed him of the charges of murder that had been brought against him.[37]

THE PROSECUTION'S CASE

On the surface it seemed as though the prosecution had a very strong case against the four Apache defendants. Prosecutor J. D. McCabe introduced fifteen white and four Apache witnesses, many of whom provided testimony about the crime scene and the trail of the killers; one rancher knew something about the movements of the accused on the day of the killing. The prosecutor's case was also strengthened because the defendants were within twelve miles of the scene of the crime on the day of the killing. Further, Al Sieber and his Apache scouts provided detailed information about the trail of the killers, who had moved south to the Salt River and beyond. Finally, the prosecution produced two maps that illustrated the crime scene and the route that the killers had traveled after committing the crime. These maps provided the prosecution with empirical data that suggested that they had thoroughly investigated and understood the crime scene. These drawings also would help the prosecutor to convince the jury that their theory about how the crime had been committed and the identity of the killers was indeed correct. In other words, these maps and diagrams tended to authenticate the unquestioned authority of the prosecutor's evidence. In prosecuting this murder case, McCabe carefully focused his attention on the crime scene and the movement of the four defendants. If he could convince the jurors that this evidence was overwhelming against the four defendants, he would win his case. Equally important, the prosecutor had what we now commonly call the race card: The accused were Apaches and the victim white, in nineteenth-century Arizona, with an all-white jury; conviction seemed inevitable.

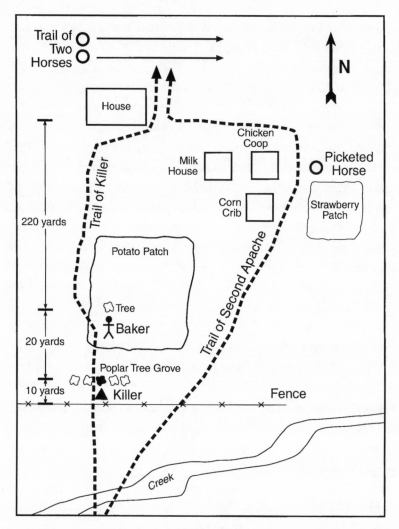

Murder scene at Baker's ranch in the Sierra Ancha Mountains, 1890.

Courtesy of Melodie Tune, graphic artist, Instructional Technology Services,
San Diego State University.

The trial began in the Gila County courthouse, Globe, Arizona, on Saturday, October 25, 1890, at 9 a.m., with the court clerk's reading of the indictment; all four defendants pled not guilty. The trial recessed and continued on Sunday, October 26, when all witnesses for the prosecution were called and sworn and ordered to remain outside until called to testify.[38] After the jury impaneling was completed, the prosecutor McCabe began to call witnesses to methodically examine the crime scene and explain how the murder had been committed. He called J. H. Baker, the father of the victim, to the stand as his first witness.

Baker testified that his son Edward had been killed on Saturday, July 12. When he arrived at the farm, he found his son's body lying about 220 yards from the house near the summit of the Sierra Ancha Mountains. Then Baker explained his son's movements on that day, noting that, after leaving the house, Edward had passed by the milk house to reach the potato patch where he was working. J. H. Baker, accompanied by George Shute, Robert Knowles, Wallace Kenton Hinton, and Baker's other son John, examined the body. They found Edward lying face down with a gunshot wound in the back; the bullet had exited around the navel. The prosecution produced a map of the crime scene that, with instructions from J. H. Baker, had been drawn by another man at the Baker homestead. After some discussion among counsel, the court accepted the use of this map and a map that illustrated the killer's trail as court exhibits while the witness gave his testimony. The witness was asked if he recognized the crime scene map. Baker replied, "Yes," and pointed to the stump where "an Indian was secreted behind" at the time of the shooting. Baker showed on the map where the moccasin tracks led from the stump, about thirty feet away, right up to the body of the deceased.[39] The somewhat elaborate map depicted the house, milk house, strawberry patch, chicken coop, corn crib, creek, meadow, and then, due south of the house, the potato patch and the tree that the victim had been chopping. The stump where the killer had been hiding was located about sixty feet farther south and, beyond that about thirty feet was the fence. Baker and the other ranchers discovered two sets of moccasin prints that had been left in the ploughed potato field. The attackers apparently came from the creek, approached the house over hard ground, killed their victim, then entered the house, found a variety of items, and threw what they did not want out on the porch and on the ground. Through Baker's testimony, the prosecution had thoroughly described the crime scene and documented the movements of the killers, and, equally important, McCabe had helped to add veracity and authenticity to the maps that were being used to present his case against the defendants.

According to Baker's testimony, the stolen, unshod horse had been used for plowing and was taken north around the house, and about one hundred yards from there the killers' tracks met with other horse tracks and "went off together." Baker and others followed the trail east to Knowles's ranch, about a mile away, and then continued on three miles before reaching Cherry Creek.[40] The killers then turned south along the creek another nine miles until it passed near Patterson's house, continued on for about six miles, and then passed within four miles of Pringle's ranch before turning east to Coon Creek, then south five miles to the Salt River. The distance from Baker's house to Patterson's was about twelve miles. Baker found the stolen frying pan on the road south of Patterson's on Cherry Creek about a quarter mile from Pringle's.

During cross-examination by W. H. Griffin, Baker claimed that the horse tracks of the killers were *all shod*, and with small shoes, suggesting ponies. Baker described the stolen horse as weighing about eleven hundred pounds, dark brown with a small star on his forehead, carrying a J.B. brand on the left shoulder with a small "x" near the brand—and unshod.[41]

Prosecutor J. D. McCabe next called Edward B. Ingalls and asked him how far his ranch was from the site of the killing. Ingalls replied that it was "about a mile and a half." Ingalls testified that another man had passed by the Baker place and saw the clothes and guns lying on the porch and in the yard and reported it to him. On Monday, July 14, Ingalls investigated and found Baker lying dead, facedown. He immediately went over to the senior Baker's ranch to inform J. H. of the shooting.[42] George Shute stated that he, Wallace Kenton Hinton, and Baker examined the body. He admitted that he and others had been tracking around the site so much "I couldn't discern whether it was our tracks or moccasin tracks."[43] Robert S. Knowles, the next witness, testified that when he arrived at the crime scene, J. H. Baker, Shute, John Baker Jr., Ingalls, and Griffin were already there. After looking at the prosecutor's map (Exhibit A), Knowles said, "We came in at this gap south of the ranch, and found Baker's body in front of this tree."[44] By this time, however, Al Sieber and his Apache scouts had arrived, and they trailed the killers about four hundred yards and found some of Baker's papers from the trunk lying along the trail. Knowles, Baker, and Samuels followed Sieber and the scouts to Patterson's place, about ten miles, and then lost the trail.[45]

S. S. Patterson proved to be one of the most important witnesses for the prosecution. He testified that he had been out gathering livestock on the Wednesday before the killing when he noticed "Indian signs around" his own house, but didn't think too much about it because he had not actually seen any Indians. The next day around noon he saw Bakelcle, one of the defendants. Patterson put on his "six shooter" and went out to talk to him. The defendant asked if he could stop for a while because it was raining and Patterson said yes. He received some venison from Bakelcle, and they both went into the house. They were conversing in English and the defendant spoke some Spanish as well, which Patterson could not understand.[46] Bakelcle claimed to be part of Guadalupe's group, which had gone to San Carlos but was coming back in two days. The witness knew Guadalupe and stated that he had gone to San Carlos eight or ten days before. During the trial, Patterson admitted that he did not understand much of what Bakelcle had said to him during their conversation, but understood that he would return with "his wife and children with him to gather fruit and walnuts." Bakelcle stayed at Patterson's until about 3 or 4 p.m. When the rain stopped, he left, riding south "on the Globe and Pleasant Valley trail towards Globe and Pringle's."[47] Patterson did not see him again until the trial.

On Saturday, Patterson got up and saw three Indian men and three women who had made a camp on Cherry Creek near his ranch. Natsin and his brother stayed in the camp while Batdish and a woman left. Natsin came to the house and spoke with Patterson. The witness said Natsin spoke good English. Patterson also gave a vest to Natsin, who had been known as "Dandy Jim" among the ranchers in that area along Cherry Creek.[48] Around noon Patterson rode over to the Apache camp and found only one man there; later, at about 6 p.m., he went over again; they were packing up to leave. They apparently had killed two deer up in the Sierra Ancha Mountains. Asked to show where their camp had been on the map (Exhibit B), he showed his house, the Globe and Pleasant Valley Trail, Pringle's, "up here about three-quarters of a mile is where they were camped, up on the other side of the creek."[49] Patterson claimed that there was a dividing ridge between Coon Creek and Cherry Creek. Guadalupe's camp was about three-quarters of a mile from Patterson's house, three to four miles from

Pringle's. The Apaches had a gray mule, a colt, and Indian ponies that were unshod. They had been camped there about three days and maintained a fire in the camp.[50]

During cross-examination, Griffin asked him how far it was from his ranch to the Baker homestead. Patterson answered, "It is about ten miles I judge." The witness claimed that the scouts had been following the trail of a barefooted horse, but the trail did not go into the Apache camp and instead crossed over toward Pringle's place. Patterson admitted that he was well acquainted with "Jim and Guadalupe," who had been up there frequently "among the ranchers."[51] Prosecutor McCabe had used Patterson to document the movements of Guadalupe and his sons prior to and on the day of the killing. He had convincing evidence that the defendants might have gone up into the Sierra Ancha Mountains, killed two deer, and while they were at it, murdered Baker.

Next, the prosecutor began to further corroborate the movements of the four defendants. McCabe called William H. Beard and asked him if he knew the defendants. He replied that he had his camp about "six or seven miles from Patterson's, just on the line of the Reservation," where he had been "holding a herd of cattle up on the Salt River just at the edge of the Reservation."[52] Around June 29, he saw the four defendants along with two other men, a boy, and several women; Beard knew that they belonged to Guadalupe's band. Beard had hired Pringle to help him with the cattle, along with Dick Baker and another hand. They had been rounding up cattle around Cherry Creek that day and got back near dusk. He was approached by Natsin, who advised them that because they were on reservation land, "we must move the cattle from that place." The next morning they began to move the cattle west across the reservation line. Natsin came by, saying they were headed for "Roggenstrau's on Salt River to gather saguaro fruit near the mouth of Coon Creek."[53] Later that day, one of the defendants came up; Beard heard him, jumped up, and walked to the door with a six-shooter. "Jim Dandy [Natsin] asked for something to eat, and I gave him what cold grub we had." Beard asked him if he was going to Roggenstrau's, and he said no, he was going to camp over by Sombrero Butte. After he left, Beard followed him for a while, and he went in the opposite direction from Sombrero Butte. Beard stated that the defendants were at "Frenchy's on the evening of the 7th and on the morning of the 8th I followed them right down the trail."

During cross-examination, Griffin asked if they were on Cherry Creek. Beard replied yes, "they went down to Pringle's ranch in the neighborhood of six miles, and there the trail takes across over there in that direction over to Coon Creek."[54] Beard had corroborated that the defendants had been at Patterson's and also stated that they had lied to him about their movements, suggesting that they would be unreliable witnesses.

Prosecutor McCabe called Al Sieber, chief of the Apache scouts. Sieber testified that after a journey from San Carlos requiring twenty-four hours, he had arrived at the crime scene on Wednesday, July 16. Sieber stated that the area around the body had been "trampled" by people walking around the area. His scouts, however, found three tracks but could not determine if three people had made them. Sieber trailed the killer to two different camps. The scouts discovered two sets of moccasin prints and "trailed them past Knowles' and then [they] split off" in different directions.[55] It rained, and the scouts were unable to find the two moccasin prints the next day, but they were able to trail the horse tracks left by the killers.

During cross-examination, Griffin asked Sieber about the methods of tracking. He said that his scouts usually dismount when they are trailing. Sieber testified that after leaving Baker's homestead, the killers struck due east over a divide. This was familiar territory for Sieber: "I understand the country thoroughly, been all over it hundreds of times." At the top of the mountain from Knowles's, "they struck for the top of the mountain, due east." Sieber said, "Now right here, opposite Look Out Peak, is where the two moccasin tracks came in; right here on the top of the mountain is where the track of another horse came in, and the horse lost a shoe."[56] After about three hours' tracking they found the horse trail again, which they followed to within six miles of Patterson's ranch. At that point they found some bullet molds thrown away by the killers. Sieber testified that "the scouts all said it was Massai did the killing."[57]

Griffin then asked Sieber about the first camp. Sieber stated that it was about one to one and a half miles away from Baker's; the killers had been there for one night. The second camp was discovered about twelve miles away from the first, or about six miles from Patterson's ranch. The lone killer—they had lost the trail of the others—had stopped two nights there. He had left that camp and continued "parallel with Coon Creek, going through Patterson's cattle ranch." They traveled farther to Coon Creek, where they lost the trail. Sieber claimed that the distance from Baker's to Coon Creek was about twenty-three miles.[58]

To buttress Sieber's testimony, the prosecutor called on Jetanaki, a corporal of the San Carlos Apache scouts, to testify. He was with Al Sieber at Baker's homestead, where they found two sets of moccasin tracks that went toward the house and one barefooted track that led from the house to the tree where they found the deceased. They picked up the trail that was headed toward Knowles's place. They were trailing three mounts: a pony and two big horses, one unshod. All three tracks were made the same day that Baker was killed, and they left at the same time. It rained, so the next day the men went back to pick up the trail and discovered where one man had camped just two miles from Baker's house. They followed the trail down a ravine and, near Patterson's ranch, they found another campsite where the killer had eaten. The next day, they followed the trail down Coon Creek to the Salt River, crossed it, and stopped following it near Black Mountain.[59] Asked the distance from where the one man had camped to where he had eaten, Jetanaki estimated thirteen miles. This was near where the trail crossed over from Cherry Creek west to Coon Creek before heading south to the Salt River. During cross-examination, Griffin asked Jetanaki if they followed the horse with one shoe missing all the way to the Salt River. Jetanaki answered, "Yes sir." The horse and rider had crossed into Coon Creek a little above where it entered the Salt River.[60]

John Daisy, another Apache scout, corroborated that they had trailed three horses from the scene of the crime to Knowles's place. They followed the three mounts for about one and a half miles from Baker's before they split up. They continued following the horse. At this point Judge Kibbey, who was presiding, became somewhat exasperated about this dwelling on testimony about trailing and asked, "What's the use of all this?" Prosecutor J. D. McCabe retorted, "Trailing the parties. It is all circumstantial evidence. Showing where they went to, and how they moved generally." The court: "What difference does it make where they stopped?" McCabe: "It is very long, but it may be material."[61] John Daisy testified that after the trail came out of Coon Creek they followed it south to the Salt River. They knew it was the correct trail because the horse had a shoe missing.[62]

The prosecutor next called Richard Baker, brother of the deceased, and asked him what he knew about the killers' trail. On the day of the crime he was at Frenchy's ranch on Cherry Creek. Later, they followed horse tracks south down Cherry

Creek from Frenchy's to Patterson's ranch, a distance of seven miles, and eventually reached Pringle's ranch. About three miles from Frenchy's, he noticed a horse track going up Cherry Creek. There were one shod and two unshod horses. It was about four miles from Pringle's. He saw the track that looked like the brown horse that had been stolen on the Salt River.[63] During cross-examination, Baker claimed that he saw the stolen horse's track along the Salt River on the trail from the Redmond ranch to Wheatfields. J. D. McCabe for the prosecution rested his case.

The contradictory testimony by the prosecution witnesses on where the two trails led is very hard to follow and tends to leave the reader baffled. You can imagine that the jury also found this testimony very confusing. It may have had an important impact on their final decision.

THE DEFENSE'S CASE

Judge Joseph H. Kibbey had appointed W. H. Griffin and P. B. McCabe to defend the four Apaches. In these types of murder cases, court-appointed legal counsel usually received a nominal fee to defend their clients.[64] The exact date they were appointed is unknown; usually it occurred when the defendants were brought into court for the first time. Whatever the date, Griffin and McCabe started at a great disadvantage because they normally practiced civil law and had little time or resources to prepare their defense. Preparation for a murder trial demands careful planning to make sure that the client's rights are protected and to ensure that he or she receives a fair trial. A thorough examination of all the evidence and a walk-through of the crime scene would normally take place to make sure they had not missed anything. That, of course, was impossible in this particular case because of time limitations and the remote location of the crime scene. It would have been logical and essential for defense counsel to advance an alternative theory to explain why the defendant could not have committed the crime. Because no records of the court-appointed attorneys exist, and because the opening statements and trial summations were not part of the trial transcript, we can only speculate how the defense lawyers began their case. The requirements to prepare a complete defense would have been very difficult to achieve in such a short time frame and with poorly-paid, inexperienced lawyers. A careful reading of the trial transcript indicates that none of these suggested steps were taken by defense counsel.

W. H. Griffin, assisted by P. B. McCabe, took on a difficult task in agreeing to defend the four Apaches. Although tribal or band affiliation was unknown, Guadalupe, age fifty, had been employed as a scout at Fort Apache, as had his two sons, Batdish and Natsin, ages twenty and twenty-three. They had been working in that capacity for several years, suggesting that they had bought into the changes brought about by the U.S. Army in Arizona Territory. In other words, they accepted and supported the white culture that had taken control of Fort Apache and San Carlos. Bakelcle, age thirty-three, probably did not belong to Guadalupe's band, and there is little employment information about him, although it is known that he worked for white ranchers on occasion, herding cattle and locating stray horses.

Griffin presented the case for the defense calling just the four defendants and one white witness to testify. This proved to be the weakest link in the defense counsel's strategy. By placing the defendants on the stand, Griffin opened them up to cross-examination that included conflicting testimony, which may have suggested that they were lying and actually may have killed Baker. The use of Marejildo Grijalva to interpret from Apache to Spanish to English also proved to be problematic. There were numerous occasions when English words must have been put into the mouths of the defendants because it was not typical language that they would have used. This translation by Grijalva seemed to create poor or even misleading information about them.

Griffin first called Guadalupe to testify. Guadalupe claimed that he knew nothing about the killing of Baker; however, he admitted that he had been camped "near where this man was killed." He testified that he had been at Patterson's one evening, then started off to his camp at Cibicue, and arrived home in two days. He and others had camped near Patterson's while picking saguaro fruit. He and Natsin and Batdish, his two sons, followed deer tracks up into the Sierra Ancha Mountains, where they killed and butchered two deer. He remembered that Patterson came up to their camp as they were packing and about to leave. Natsin went back to Patterson's house with him. They next camped above Pringle's in a "big bunch of cotton-wood trees" for one night and then continued on north and east. They crossed Canyon Creek, traveled to a big hill, and camped there for one night. They arrived at Cibicue the next evening. That was all that he knew.[65]

During cross-examination by prosecutor McCabe, Guadalupe claimed that they left Pringle's and traveled north up Cherry Creek, camping three nights on their return journey to Cibicue. Guadalupe admitted that he had been wearing a vest given to his son Natsin by Patterson. He denied seeing Bakelcle on the mountain and claimed that he was not in his camp the day they were camped at Patterson's ranch; however, he did see Bakelcle at Cibicue after returning home. He admitted that he camped two nights near Pringle's, and then "he came down towards Salt River and stayed three nights before he turned back towards home."[66] He said he first heard about the killing from Lieutenant Jones at Camp Apache—that was about seven to ten days later. He denied telling "Al Sieber at San Carlos that

Bakelcle came down to his camp on Coon Creek." Guadalupe also denied that Bakelcle had come into his camp. He admitted that he had camped with him at San Carlos, but said he did not see him again until Cibicue.[67] Under cross-examination, Guadalupe's testimony appeared to be confused, possibly because of the interpreter, or he could have been lying. Nevertheless, the jurors certainly must have picked up on this during the prosecutor's questioning and probably began to draw conclusions about the veracity of the defendant.

Griffin next called Bakelcle. Bakelcle claimed that he first heard about the killing from the scouts who arrested him. Griffin: "Do you know anything about it?" Bakelcle: "No, sir."[68] During cross-examination, he admitted to knowing Patterson and that he was in his house. Turning to the interpreter, Griffin said, "Ask him if he heard Lupe's testimony about his having a gun in his camp up on the Cibicu?" Grijalva said, "He says he had a needle gun, caliber 50, a three-band gun; he got it from a white man; it was a 15 cartridge gun; he brought in three stray horses to this man and the man gave him this gun." Asked to explain, Grijalva replied that he said, "Yes, sir; it was over by John Dazen's camp; this man that gave him this gun is here; he saw him here."[69] He did not know the man's name. It was a fairly new gun that had not been used much. He told Griffin that he did not accompany Guadalupe and his group from Patterson's to Cibicue; he arrived there before them. He did not have the gun when he was at Patterson's ranch. He acquired the gun after he returned home to Cibicue. A white man came to him and asked him to search for horses and he received the gun in payment. He claimed that he did not know Baker or where Baker's ranch was located. Bakelcle also claimed that about nine days after that he returned home and visited John Dazen's camp. While there, two Apache scouts arrived and told him about the killing of Baker; they were going in search of the killers.[70]

Defense called Martin Gentry and, without the need for the interpreter, asked him whether he had seen Bakelcle in "June or the first of July" at John Dazen's camp. Gentry testified that he did and that he asked Bakelcle to hunt some stray horses for him. He came to Gentry's house twice and brought the stray horses after about five days. In payment he gave him "a gun; it was 'Long Tom' style needle gun; it was a 50 caliber." Asked if Bakelcle had a gun when he first came to Gentry's place, Gentry replied that he had a "44 carbine Winchester; he had no cartridges for his gun at all." He heard about the Baker killing, and about eight to ten days after that he gave Bakelcle the gun.[71] The prosecutor recalled Guadalupe and asked him "if he and another Indian came through Globe here to a camp near town, one of them on an iron grey mule and another one on a dark bay horse with a white spot on its forehead." Guadalupe replied through the interpreter, "No; he says he never been here before for a good while; he says he lives on the Cibicu and never comes here at all."[72]

Defense counsel then called Batdish, with Grijalva interpreting. Batdish claimed that he knew nothing about the Baker killing. During cross-examination, Batdish admitted that he heard about it from the commanding officer over at Camp Apache. Batdish, a scout, had gone to Camp Apache to get paid; that is when he heard about the killing. He admitted that he had been camping with Guadalupe at Patterson's. They had three unshod Indian ponies and a shod mule. Asked about his job, he replied through the interpreter, "Yes, he was in the scouts then at the time; he was in the service then."[73]

Griffin asked Natsin, his next witness, whether he knew anything about the Baker killing. He said no. During cross-examination, Natsin stated that he went to Camp Apache with his father and brother. That was where he heard about the killing, when Lieutenant Jones told his father. He testified that he, his father, and his brother had traveled north up Canyon

Creek to reach Cibicue. Soon after he went to Camp Apache with his father and brother. His "father was arrested" after he had returned to Cibicue.[74] At this point Griffin stated that the defense would rest; they had called their last witness and had completed their argument for the defendants. Considering the seriousness of the charges, the defense strategy seems short-sighted and certainly lacking.

THE VERDICT

During rebuttal, the prosecution called Lieutenant Jones, who had been assigned to investigate the murder case. Asked if he knew Patterson and if he understood Apache, Jones replied, "I understand a few words, not sufficient to understand any or to carry on conversation." He said that there was no indication that "Lupe recognized Patterson up to the time of the recognition of the vest." Asked what took place then, Jones replied, "The investigation seemed to have proceeded as far as I could carry it. There was a lull. Then Patterson asked Lupe where he got that vest; I told the interpreter to ask Lupe where he got that vest and he said—" Griffin objected. The court asked, "Do you know of your own knowledge whether he [Guadalupe] was on or off the Reservation at the time the killing occurred?" Jones: "I do not, not of my knowledge; I do, from what he said through the interpreter."[75] Asked if the interpreter was in court, J. D. McCabe answered, "No, sir; we telegraphed for him and he is said to have started; Mickey Free is the gentleman; I will ask stringent measures against him after the case is closed."[76] The court would not allow the testimony without the scout. Lieutenant Jones testified that he made the arrest about "32 days after the murder."[77] Prosecutor McCabe closed his rebuttal.

Judge Kibbey asked defense counsel, "You have no instructions?" Griffin replied, "No, sir: submit the Court to give such instructions as it desires."[78] With testimony closed, the case was argued to the jury by counsel, after which the court instructed the jury as to murder, accessories to the crime, malice, presumption of innocence resting with defendants, and reasonable doubt. Robert Samuels was sworn in as bailiff to take charge of the jury; they retired at 5 p.m. on Monday, October 27, to consider their verdict. Later that evening (time unknown), the jury returned with a verdict of guilty for all four defendants. Judge Kibbey sentenced all of them to life in prison for murder, to be served at the Yuma Territorial Prison.

THE APPEAL

On January 8, 1891, W. H. Griffin and P. B. McCabe, attorneys for the defendants, filed a brief and argument to the Supreme Court of the Territory of Arizona, requesting that the verdicts of the four defendants be overturned. They began with a discussion of evidence, claiming that if it "fails to meet the allegations in the indictment, that is, the charge in the indictment, then, and in that case, the conviction is not sustained by the proofs."[79] Defense counsel argued that "if the evidence offered by the prosecution fails to prove that Batdish" had killed Baker on July 12, 1890, "then this conviction is not supported by the evidence. If the evidence fails to show that Bakelcle, Guadalupe, and Natsin were present on the 12th day of July, 1890, and aided and assisted Batdish in the murder of Edward Baker, then, in that case, the conviction of these men is not supported by the evidence. This is the issue that defendants present to this Court."[80]

The defense began to explain the facts about the killing of Baker on his "potato and milk ranch, on the summit of the Sierra Ancha range of mountains." The victim was last seen alive on Friday, July 11, and neighbors discovered his body on Monday, July 14, about two hundred yards from the house, near a large pine tree. He had been shot in the back "and his head nearly severed from the trunk, with an ax."[81] The evidence suggested that he had been killed on the afternoon of Saturday, July 12. The killers took two guns and a large unshod horse. The evidence stated that there were moccasin tracks and at least two were distinct around the body, and that these tracks led to the house. Those who discovered the body buried it. On July 16, five days after the killing, Al Sieber and his Indian scouts arrived to track the killers. Then the attorneys described the rugged nature of the Sierra Ancha Mountains. Cherry Creek, a long mountain stream, just east of the mountains, ran north and south, emptying into the Salt River, and Coon Creek, farther west, also ended up in the Salt River. A series of ranches were located along Cherry Creek, including those of Patterson, Pringle, and Gentry. "The main trail runs along the course of Cherry Creek," and this region borders the western side of San Carlos and Fort Apache reservations.[82]

The prosecution tried to connect Guadalupe, Batdish, and Natsin to the crime because they, along with two women, a boy, and a girl, had appeared "at Patterson's ranch on Cherry Creek" about seven or eight in the morning of Saturday, July 12. Patterson got up and prepared breakfast and Natsin stayed to eat breakfast with him. Guadalupe's family camped near Coon Creek, and Patterson visited their camp about noon. Later, around 5 p.m., Patterson visited them again and "saw nothing unusual about the camp, except he thought packing was rather hastily done."[83] They were getting ready to take the trail to Cibicue, near Fort Apache. Defense counsel claimed the prosecution theorized that Batdish, Guadalupe, and Natsin left Patterson's place, went to the ranch, killed Baker, and returned to their camp on Patterson's ranch before 6 p.m. and then left. The prosecution claimed that their hasty retreat indicated "an effort to avoid detection." Patterson, however, had been in the camp, talked to the men, and "saw nothing unusual; did not see

Baker's horse" and none "of Baker's property in possession of these defendants."[84]

After briefly explaining the accusations by the prosecution and the basic facts of the crime, defense counsel turned to the main contradictory evidence. Their basic argument focused on Al Sieber and his scouts, who found and followed the trail left by the killers as they moved south toward the Salt River. Counsel explained that the Apache scouts "are composed of trusty and experienced trailers, and woodsmen. If any testimony in relation to a trail, or trailing, can be relied on in Court, surely Sieber, and his scouts, are first class evidence."[85] The defense reiterated the various accounts given by the scouting party in order to demonstrate that they had followed the true killer's trail.

In his testimony, J. H. Baker said that "it took him three and one half hours to make the trip, down the mountain, on the most direct route." Sieber testified that he went to Baker's ranch, his scouts "picked up the trail very quick," and headed toward Knowles's place. The scouts located "three horse tracks, two large, and one small; one was shod."[86] The scouts followed the trail east, in a roundabout way, for about four miles, and found a camp where one of the killers stayed all night. Just before they discovered the overnight camp, the scouts lost the trail of the unshod ponies. They followed the shod horse's trail, which "wound round the mountain for about twelve or thirteen miles" to where the killer camped all night again. This second "camp was about six or seven miles from Patterson's ranch."[87] Jetanaki testified that they continued to follow the trail south to the Salt River, "then followed it towards Wheatfields, south, on until it turned up into the Black mountains, where they left the trail." That would be at least sixty miles or more. Defense counsel argued that despite some minor differences between Sieber's and the scouts' testimony, "the proof is quite clear that the scouts followed the correct trail directly from the scene of the murder to where they dropped it."[88]

In a discussion of the shod horse that the scouts had been following, defense counsel noted that J. H. Baker testified that his stolen animal "was a very large *bare-footed horse. We didn't shoe him; we used him for cultivating.* From this, it would appear that the shod horse the scouts followed, was not Baker's horse." Baker's horse had been taken by the two Apaches who "soon separated from the lone shod horse, followed by the scouts."[89] Turning to the maps used by the prosecution, defense counsel argued that "the Court will observe, that the trail, as followed from Baker's ranch, in the direction of Patterson's ranch, and left in the Black mountains, did not go to the camp of Guadalupe, near the Patterson ranch, but passed down Coon Creek, on the opposite side from Guadalupe's camp, and never did connect with Guadalupe's trail."[90] They argued that the evidence indicates that "if Guadalupe and his boys, on their mule and Indian ponies, had come down from Baker's ranch, after the killing, on Saturday, the 12th, they could not have escaped the vigilance of these scouts. Or, if this trail from Baker's ranch, the shod horse had have gone into Guadalupe's camp, then there might be some excuse for the detention and conviction of these defendants." The attorneys contended that the verdict of the jury was not supported by the evidence; in fact, it "establishes the innocence of the three defendants, Natsin, Batdish, and Guadalupe."[91] If they had killed Baker, why didn't these tracks lead to Guadalupe's camp? The evidence reveals that the trail from the murder scene at Baker's ranch never entered Guadalupe's camp. The scouts followed the killer's trail south along Coon Creek where it passed three to four miles east of Guadalupe's camp near Patterson's ranch and continued on to the Gila River. It seemed clear to defense counsel that this fact alone would indicate their innocence. They argued that "we rely strictly on the evidence of Sieber, and his two scouts. We consider it the only reliable testimony" on the trails that lead from Baker's ranch.[92]

Defense noted that "Guadalupe and these defendants, could not have slept two nights on the trail from Baker's to within six or seven miles of Patterson's ranch, where the last camp was made. . . . These circumstances alone" proved that the defendants could not have committed the murder because they were "camped at Patterson's ranch, between eight o'clock in the morning, and six in the evening."[93] Sieber had found a horseshoe that had come from the shod horse they were tracking. He showed it to J. H. Baker, who said that "it did not come off his horse."[94] Consequently, the horse they were trailing was not Baker's stolen horse.

The attorneys then turned to Guadalupe's testimony about where and when he camped, which seemed contradictory. They claimed that although the "Court ruled out this testimony," the jury "took it in for all it was worth, and more." Guadalupe had been interrogated in the Indian agent's office in the presence of several others, including Patterson. Later, after being taken to Globe, the district attorney questioned Guadalupe with Grijalva acting as interpreter. This should have been inadmissible.

> The persistent efforts of the District Attorney to force this kind of testimony before the jury, had its effect. He went so far as to plead with the Court, and finally took exceptions, or refusal to allow the testimony to come in, a thing the prosecution has no right to do on criminal trials. This zeal, displayed before the jury, no doubt, impressed them with the idea that the Court was in error, and the District Attorney right.

Defense counsel argued that the jury "considered these contradictions as evidence" and failed to observe "the order of the

Court excluding it." They continued, "We have no doubt that the exceptions of the District Attorney to the ruling of the Court, on these admissions, so-called, had more influence with the jury than all the evidence in the case, and, no doubt, brought about the conviction of all these defendants.[95]

Turning to Bakelcle, the fourth defendant, they note that he was arrested and accused of involvement in the killing of Baker and that his gun "was a Long Tom, fifty caliber, of the same kind Baker lost from the ranch." During the trial, however, when Bakelcle "was undergoing a most rigid cross-examination," he saw the man who had given him the gun in the courtroom. Defense counsel then called Martin Gentry to testify. Gentry's testimony exonerated the defendant and "show[ed] that he let him have the gun about the time of the murder of Baker. This exploded that suspicion, for there was no proof that the gun was Baker's." The defendant's story was "corroborated by Beard's and Gentry's testimony."[96] Bakelcle "hunted, killed a deer, gave Patterson a ham, ate dinner with him, was riding a bare-foot pony, with a colt following." He left Patterson's, traveled to Cibicue, located and returned Gentry's lost horses, and received the gun as payment. Bakelcle "remained at home until he was arrested." Finally, defense counsel argued "that there is not one word of testimony to support this conviction, and the judgment should be in all things set aside, and these defendants discharged."[97] After considering this appeal, the Supreme Court of the Territory of Arizona affirmed the judgment of the court.[98]

FINAL OBSERVATIONS

The final outcome of the trial and appeal of Batdish, Bakelcle, Guadalupe, and Natsin needs to be examined further. Considering the evidence, the testimony, and the arguments presented by the prosecutor and defense counsel, the verdict and affirmation by the Supreme Court of the Territory of Arizona might seem troubling to the reader. The jury's verdict, however, can be explained by a variety of factors. Certainly the poor defense helps to account for the conviction. The defense had called the four Apache defendants, and thus they had opened up their clients to a sharp and damaging cross-examination that revealed conflicting testimony. And, of course, Batdish, Bakelcle, Guadalupe, and Natsin were difficult to understand because of the need to translate from Apache to Spanish to English. It is possible that under the difficult circumstances, such as insufficient time to prepare their case, the failure to provide an alternative hypothesis, and lack of funds to investigate the circumstances of the crime, it was the best defense they could provide. What proves to be most puzzling, however, is the failure to broach the issue of circumstantial evidence during the trial instead of tacking on several California case law references at the end of the appeal's brief and argument in their attempt to overturn the verdicts. For example, during the trial they could have cited *People v. Shuler,* an 1865 California case that cautioned against relying heavily on circumstantial evidence. They could have requested that Judge Kibbey instruct the jury that while using circumstantial evidence they must be cautious. The *People v. Shuler* ruling states, "It is always insufficient to convict or warrant a verdict, when assuming all to be proved with evidence tends to prove, some other hypothesis may still be true."[99] Two other cases clarify and buttress this legal premise. In *People v. Strong,* the presiding court judge refused to give defense counsel's arguments about relying on circumstantial evidence to the jury. One of the defense counsel's requests read, "Circumstantial evidence is always insufficient to convict; when conceding all to be proved that the evidence tends to prove, some other hypothesis than that of the defendant's guilt may be true." The California Supreme Court cited Simon Greenleaf's (a noted authority on legal evidence) argument: "Where a criminal charge is to be proved by circumstantial evidence, the proof ought to be not only consistent with the prisoner's guilt, but inconsistent with every other rational conclusion."[100] In a similar case (*People v. Dick*) the following year, the California Supreme Court further clarified this issue.[101] In all three cases they overturned the verdicts and sent them back for retrial. If the defense counsel for Batdish, Bakelcle, Guadalupe, and Natsin had used this argument during the trial, and requested that the court instruct the jury to heed this legal advice on circumstantial evidence, the results might have been different. The evidence about the killer's trail that passed Patterson's ranch without entering Guadalupe's camp, and that continued on south to the Salt River, provides an obvious alternative hypothesis that absolves the defendants of guilt.

There were significant weaknesses in the evidence and testimony presented by the prosecution. Although some witnesses were effective, others provided conflicting testimony that could have hurt the prosecution's case if it had been pursued and attacked by the defense. For example, the prosecution's evidence involving the killer's trail certainly was contradictory. If Guadalupe killed Baker, why didn't the trail lead to his camp near Patterson's ranch? If Bakelcle received his gun from Gentry sometime after the killing, that would document that he did not steal Baker's gun and could not have killed him. Why did the defense fail to attack the prosecution's lack of motive? The defendants had been employed for many years as scouts—why would they kill a rancher in an isolated area and rob him? It did not make sense. If Guadalupe had indeed killed Baker, where was the horse and stolen items taken from the victim? Patterson admitted that he did not see anything unusual in Guadalupe's camp, such as Baker's horse or other stolen property. Once again, the defendants were convicted on weak circumstantial evidence that could not place the defendants at the crime scene and failed to provide any evidence that they had taken items from Baker's homestead. Finally, Al Sieber believed that Batdish, Guadalupe, Bakelcle, and Natsin did not kill Baker. His Apache scouts told him that Massai, a Chiricahua "renegade," had committed the crime; they recognized his footprints, which they had seen before while trying to apprehend him. Apparently, Sieber, the chief of scouts, could convince no one that the four defendants were guiltless. On July 26, 1890, Globe's *Arizona Silver Belt* noted that "Mr. Sieber is entitled to his opinion, but there is nothing in the circumstances that warrants such a belief. . . . The facts . . . point strongly to [these] Cibicu Indians." The *Silver Belt* editor, however, admitted that "the evidence against them was flimsy."[102] By now the reader should be aware (as the prosecution surely was) that there were weaknesses that could have been attacked by the defense. The prosecution most likely realized that defense counsel mainly practiced civil law and would not discover and be able to exploit these weaknesses. In this assumption they were correct.

What can we conclude about the jury? They probably approximated a cross section of the white community. Although not a jury of the defendants' "peers," they were a fairly typical group of white male jurors.[103] What opinions they held about Indians, of course, remains a mystery; however, given their tendency to perceive the Indians as ruthless and cruel, and considering that the defendants were Apaches and feared by many, the jurors probably harbored prejudice and may have been hostile, especially since the victim had been a white man. Equally important, the four defendants were unable to clearly understand the language in which the trial was conducted and, because of faulty translation, were vulnerable in the Arizona territorial criminal justice system. Native Americans were at risk in a white society that viewed them as misfits and marginal outsiders; consequently, such injustices were common throughout the American West during the nineteenth century.

THE UNBALANCED SCALES OF JUSTICE

NEWSPAPER HEADLINES

Good Indians, Five Apache Murderers Gone to Glory!
The Gallows Cheated of Three of Its Victims

Arizona Weekly Enterprise, December 7, 1889

THE FOUR HOMICIDE case studies presented here have offered some insights into the treatment of Apache defendants tried before the U.S. District federal courts and the territorial courts in Arizona Territory. Whether the killings were the result of a feud, an Apache raid, the actions of a young disgruntled Apache, or an isolated murder in the Sierra Anchas, each case is unique. Consequently, these four murder trials provide very differing circumstances, yet they end with similar results—conviction of the defendants. There is, however, a series of commonalities that helps to explain why the criminal justice system failed to extend equal treatment to Apache defendants.

All of these trials were conducted by white judges, jurors, prosecutors, and defense counsels. This put the defendants at risk because most whites in Arizona had been conditioned for years to view Apaches as the most dangerous of all Indians. The earlier exploits of Ulzana and Geronimo had created fear and near hysteria among many of the white population. Because Apache defendants accused of murder received court-appointed attorneys, they were placed at a great disadvantage in the criminal justice system. Experienced criminal lawyers were not interested in such cases because they would not offer substantial remuneration. During the preliminary hearings, the judge usually selected one or more lawyers from a group of attorneys in the courtroom to handle the defense. As practicing civil law attorneys, they lacked adequate preparation for handling these complicated murder cases, which might end with convictions and the death penalty. Consequently, they failed to establish alternative hypotheses for the killings, they declined to call witnesses who could have provided testimony to show mitigating factors that might have changed the outcome of the trial, they did not adequately attack the testimony of key prosecution witnesses, and some of them chose not to appeal the death penalty cases to a higher court. The evidence suggests that the defense counsel in most of these cases were just going through the motions. The remarkably short duration of these trials provides the most damaging evidence that justice was not served. Three of these cases lasted less than a day, one as short as a half a day.[1] Keep in mind that these are first-degree murder cases, with the death penalty as a possible consequence. As will be demonstrated, these cases are not the only examples of such injustice for Native American defendants.

ARIZONA TERRITORIAL COURTS, 1880–1912

To examine the Arizona territorial criminal justice system's treatment of defendants accused of murder, Cochise, Coconino, Gila, Pima, Pinal, and Yavapai counties were selected because of their location, historical significance, racial composition, and availability of data. The main purpose was to examine a cross section of ethnic population in Arizona Territory from 1880 to 1912 to determine the fairness of the criminal justice system. Cochise, Gila, and Yavapai counties were basically mining

TABLE I

CONVICTION RATE PERCENTAGES BY COUNTY AND ETHNIC COMPOSITION

County	Anglo	Indian
Cochise	39.5%	—
Coconino	21	—
Gila	42	76.5%
Pima	37.7	71.4
Pinal	47	100
Yavapai	40.7	75

Source: Registers of Criminal Action, Cochise, Coconino, Gila, Pima, Pinal, and Yavapai counties, 1880–1912, Arizona State Archives, Phoenix

regions that often included a significant Hispanic population. Gila County, since it contained a portion of the San Carlos Reservation, also provided an important number of Indian defendants. Pima and Pinal counties offer a look at Hispanics and Indians intermixed with Anglos.[2] Not surprisingly, the largest number of Indian defendants were Apaches. They were the last group to be subdued and placed on reservations. Most of the Apache murderers were arrested in one decade, 1885–1895. After that the number of homicides committed by Apaches and other Native Americans in Arizona Territory dropped dramatically.

Anglos, with 310 cases (58 percent), make up the majority of the indictments for murder during the period under study. Hispanics contributed 153 cases (29 percent) of the indictments. The mining enterprises in several of the counties, as well as the sizeable Hispanic population in Pima County, helps to account for this. Native Americans account for 66 cases (12 percent) of the indictments.[3]

Table 1 shows the disparity of conviction rates of these six counties in Arizona Territory.[4] There were no murder cases involving Native Americans in Cochise County, and Coconino County recorded only three cases; all three were dismissed. In the remaining four counties the conviction rates of Native Americans compared to Anglos is striking.[5] It is remarkable how uniform the conviction rates are for Native Americans. In terms of numbers, Gila and Pinal counties convicted twenty-one and eight Apaches respectively. Separating the Apache defendants from other Native Americans reveals more remarkable statistics. In the six counties, fifty-four of the sixty-six Native American defendants were Apaches (82 percent). Within this group, the convictions rate was 91 percent, with just five Apache defendants receiving a not guilty verdict. The murder trials that found Apaches not guilty involved Apache victims, usually women. Apache defendants paid a high price for their crimes. White defendants' not guilty verdicts were three times the Apache rates. Finally, it seems clear that the only way an Apache defendant could be found not guilty was if he had killed an Apache victim, preferably a woman. The killing of a white victim assured conviction and a severe penalty as well.

Another measure of the bias can be seen in the number of Native Americans who were convicted on a reduced charge of manslaughter. Twenty-eight percent of the Anglos received reduced charges of manslaughter, while only 14 percent of the Native Americans were convicted on the lesser charge. Equally significant, more than 16 percent of the Anglos received a sentence of only one to five years, while 7 percent of the Native Americans were given the lesser sentence. The bias suggested by the conviction rates can be partly attributed to the hostility toward Native Americans, especially Apaches, generated by the struggle for land during the period under study. Other factors include poor defense counsel, all-white juries, and a system that did not take into account the problems faced by Native Americans trying to adapt to new societal demands.

Plea bargaining, another important criterion for assessing conviction rates, was common in Arizona Territory, at least for Native American defendants. District attorneys probably practiced it to quickly resolve a legal issue with minimal expense. The district attorneys frequently pressured Apaches to plead guilty and risk the possibility of execution.[6] In all six cases where Apache males killed Apache females, the defendants were convinced by prosecutors that they should change their pleas to guilty. Two had their charges reduced to manslaughter, while the other four received reduced sentences for pleading guilty to murder.[7] This served as a convenience for the county court system, since it avoided the expense of a trial. Twenty-four percent of the Native Americans plea bargained compared to 4.8 percent of Anglos.

One can imagine the problems that an Apache confronted while being arraigned in court. They knew very little English and interpreters sometimes made mistakes in translating from one language to the other. The misinterpretation of one or two words could have a dramatic effect on understanding what the district attorney or judge was explaining. The high rate of Native American plea bargains reveals that they were at the mercy of white justice and also suggests that the system was prejudicial.

Gila County had the highest number of homicides involving Apache defendants accused of killing white victims, and most of these occurred within a short time span. Gila County attorneys prosecuted five of these ten Apache defendants in 1889, four in 1890, and the remaining defendant in 1897. In other words, ten Apache defendants committed 100 percent of these interracial homicides within an eight-year period.[8] All ten Apache defendants indicted for killing whites were convicted. During this same period there was also a significant number of white victim homicides committed by Apaches in Pinal, Graham, and Apache counties, which, along with Gila county, bordered the San Carlos Reservation.[9] The cases involving Apache killers and Apache victims, however, are spread more evenly over the period covered. After a peak period of killings, from 1893 to 1897 (eleven cases), such violent crime declined significantly.[10]

CASADORA–CAPTAIN JACK RIVALRY

As noted earlier, feuds among the Apache sometimes continued for decades, and the drinking of tiswin often fueled and prolonged them. Not surprisingly, the Captain Jack and Casadora feud flared up again some twenty-four years after the shooting at Captain Jack's camp. On October 5, 1911, Iyehe (SJ-55), a member of Casadora's band, shot and killed Captain Jack near Peridot. When Sheriff Deputy McMurray arrived at a slaughterhouse at Rice near where Iyehe lived, "he found several Indians greatly excited through fear that Iyehe would kill them." The deputy ordered the suspect to come out of his wickiup and surrender; he gave himself into the custody of the sheriff. The deputy asked where he kept his gun, and he replied that it was hidden in some bushes. The deputy searched and found a rifle with an empty magazine. Coroner Thomas arrived and found the remains of Sisto and his wife, who had been shot and killed. Meanwhile, another coroner's jury examined Captain Jack's body at Peridot, about five miles from where Sisto was killed. The coroner noted that the sixty-five-year-old Apache chief "had been shot in the head, the bullet plowing down his back into the body, as he attempted to come out of his cabin."[11]

During testimony at the coroner's inquest, Iyehe claimed that he, Sisto, and Sisto's wife, all members of the SJ band, had been hauling wood that day and that they had been drinking tiswin and were very drunk. As they arrived at Sisto's cabin,

Sisto's wife "made motions at [Iyehe], which made him angry."
Iyehe "picked up his rifle and shot her." When Sisto tried to
take his rifle from him, "he suddenly pulled the gun out of the
grasp of Sisto and shot him in the body, killing him instantly."
Iyehe then "mounted his pony and started for the cabin of Captain Jack about 5 miles away." Captain Jack's wife testified that
Iyehe "rode up to their cabin and called out to Captain Jack to
come out." When he stepped out of the door Iyehe instantly
shot Captain Jack in the head. Turning to Captain Jack's wife,
he said, "If I had another cartridge I would kill you, too."
When Sheriff Deputy McMurray asked Iyehe why he had killed
him, he replied, "Captain Jack was an old medicine man of his
tribe; that Captain Jack had doctored several of his relatives
and his medicine was 'no good—they all dead.'"[12] This statement, of course, was untrue; Captain Jack had served as an
Apache scout but never practiced as a medicine man, and, of
course, he was not a member of Iyehe's band. It is a likely possibility that Iyehe, while under the influence of tiswin, had
remembered the killing of two of his fellow SJ band members
by Captain Jack's SC band many years before and decided to
kill him in retribution. Such feuds that survived for years were
fairly common among a wide variety of ethnic groups.[13]

District Attorney G. W. Shute indicted Iyehe for murder on
December 14, 1911, and he was defended by A. L. Harper, a
court-appointed attorney, in the District Court, Fifth Judicial
District in Gila County. Convicted of first-degree murder, the
defendant appeared for the sentencing on December 21, 1911;
Iyehe received life in prison.[14] He arrived at the Arizona Territorial Prison in Florence, Arizona, on December 24. The prison
register reveals that Iyehe was "thirty-eight, 5' 6" tall, 147 lbs,
married, had five children, could not read or write, smoked
tobacco, and occupation farmer."[15] During his tenure in prison,
Iyehe was employed as a gardener; later he was transferred to

Honor Camp at Clifton on December 6, 1916. He returned to the prison the following year. Iyehe had been praised for being "observant of the rules and regulations" and had shown good behavior. Prison officials commended Iyehe for his work both as a gardener and at the Clifton Road Camp. In a proclamation for a commutation dated August 29, 1917, Governor Thomas E. Campbell reduced his life sentence to fifteen years. Because of his good behavior, Iyehe was discharged and paroled on December 4, 1918, after serving seven years of his sentence.[16]

DOING HARD TIME IN YUMA PRISON

During the nineteenth century, Apache defendants received harsh prison terms with life sentences, and many died of consumption in federal and state prisons. An evaluation of all Arizona Territorial Prison mortality statistics reveals that Native American death rates were much higher than those of either whites or Hispanics. This was an all-too-familiar experience for Native American inmates who had been sentenced to Yuma for murder or manslaughter. Thirteen (37 percent) of the Native American inmates died, surviving an average of 4.8 years. By comparison, nine white inmates (4.3 percent) died in prison, and they survived an average of twelve years before expiring. These figures parallel similar high death rates for Native American inmates at San Quentin Prison in California.[17] For reasons that remain unclear, incarceration appeared to be a death sentence for many Indians.[18] Only a few Apache inmates survived and were eventually released from prison.

For example, Batdish, Bakelcle, Guadalupe, and Natsin, received life sentences for murdering Baker and were sent to the Arizona Territorial Prison. They arrived in Yuma on November 8, 1890, received register numbers, were searched, and were placed in cells in close confinement with other inmates, some of

Yuma Territorial Prison, 1895. Batdish and many other Apaches served their time here, often dying from consumption. *Courtesy Arizona State Library, Archives and Public Records, Phoenix, No. 98-6970.*

whom may have had various contagious diseases.[19] Natsin soon contracted consumption and was not expected to recover from the disease. Consequently, upon recommendation from the prison physician and the warden, he received a pardon from Governor Lewis Hughes on November 28, 1894.[20] He returned to the reservation, where he died a month later. Guadalupe died from lung disease in prison on January 22, 1897. Batdish also died from consumption sometime early in that same year. Finally, Bakelcle, the sole survivor of the group, came down with consumption and, since the other three defendants had either died or had been released to die at home, with the physician's recommendation and the warden's approval, he received a pardon from Governor Myron H. McCord on October 5, 1897. He was allowed to return to his home to die.[21]

Other Apaches suffered a similar fate while in the custody of federal prisons. Ilthkah and Hahskingaygahlah, both tried with Captain Jack in a federal court in Phoenix, died of consumption while they were incarcerated as federal prisoners in the Ohio State Penitentiary in Columbus. They died exactly one month apart in 1889, just three months before the U.S. Supreme Court ordered the Apache defendants released and returned to San Carlos.[22]

EXECUTING APACHES

The Nahdeizaz case offers some indication of the enmity white citizens of Arizona held for Apaches. The impending execution of Nahdeizaz drew a great deal of attention from the Arizona territorial press. One editor noted the following:

> There is, however, a Tonto Apache . . . who owing to his melancholy situation; no longer mocks the silent corridors [of the jail] with shouts of mirth or music's echoing strain. Death borders upon our birth, but he perhaps never realized the fact until twelve good and true men pronounced his doom for the murder of Lieut. Seward Mott.[23]

After spending days in the "squalid cell" in the Gila County jail, on December 27, 1889, Sheriff Jerry Ryan and deputies escorted the calm Nahdeizaz to the gallows on a cloudy, somber day. According to observers standing close to the platform, when Sheriff Ryan said good-bye to the condemned before springing the trap, Nahdeizaz replied, "Good-bye hell!"[24] Some observers believe that Nahdeizaz meant he was leaving a hell created by the white man. Deputy Sheriff D. A. Reynolds swung an axe that

Nahdeizaz before his hanging in Globe, Arizona, 1889. Notice the heavy weight suspended from the crossbar. *Courtesy Arizona State Library, Archives and Public Records, Phoenix, No. 97-6029.*

severed the rope which held the weight suspended, and Nahdeizaz shot upward to the top of the gallows frame and the recoil left the body suspended in the air. A twitching of his fingers, a slight contraction of the limbs and tremor of the body, and all was over.[25]

Actually, it was not quite that clean an execution. When the weight dropped, pulling his body up, "there was a swishing sound as Nahdeizaz's body was jerked aloft to the gallows' top. A miscalculation of slack in the hanging rope permitted the body to go too high—it crashed into the crossbar atop the scaffold, badly crushing the skull. There was a gasp of horror from among the spectators. Ryan stood as if frozen."[26]

The first legal hanging in Gila County shocked many white citizens in Globe; however, the impending execution of five

Apaches sentenced to death in neighboring Pinal County provided another dimension of both hostile white attitudes and the
executions of Apaches in Arizona Territory.

White expressions of hatred for Apaches who killed white
citizens, and the strong desire to destroy these Apaches, could
be quite shocking. Pinal County officials tried, convicted, and
ordered the execution of Gonshayee, Kahdoslah, Askisaylala,
Nahconquisay, and Pahslagosla. The circumstances surrounding
the final demise of Gonshayee and his fellow Apaches require
further comment. On the eve of their execution, Gonshayee,
Askisaylala, and Pahslagosla all committed suicide in the Pinal
County Jail in Florence.[27] They tore strips from their breach
clothes

> and passed them around their necks. They then tied a secure
> knot by giving an extra twist, whereby, when once drawn
> tight, it could not be loosened, even if the victim felt so dis-
> posed. The ends of the strings were then taken by the hands of
> the suicidal aborigines and drawn tightly with a sudden jerk;
> strangulation followed.[28]

The next day, a gray, rainy morning, when authorities executed Nahconquisay and Kahdoslah, both exhibited visible
signs of being badly shaken by the news that their fellow SI
band members had committed suicide. One day after the executions, the *Arizona Weekly Enterprise* ran the following banner
headline announcing the Apache deaths: "Good Indians, Five
Apache Murderers Gone to Glory!" However, some of the
white population in Florence, robbed of retribution by the sui-
cides of Gonshayee and two of his companions, became
enraged. The night after the hangings, some of the more sadistic
Indian haters visited Gonshayee's grave site, dug up the body,
chopped off Gonshayee's head, and kept it as a souvenir. The
editor of the *Arizona Weekly Enterprise* gloated:

Nahdeizaz after his hanging in Globe, Arizona, 1889.
Courtesy Arizona State Library, Archives and Public Records, Phoenix, No. 97-6028.

Gon-sha [*sic*], the ex-chief, now lies in his grave a headless piece of clay. He cheated the gallows by committing suicide and in turn he has been cheated out of his *cabeza* . . . and to this hour it is believed that even Gon-sha has not missed the head he so mysteriously lost.

In a strong statement that was probably shared by many white Arizonans, the editor of the Flagstaff *Arizona Champion* suggested, "If there are any good Indians outside of graveyards, they do not live in Arizona."[29] This outpouring of venom against Gonshayee typifies white anger and hatred for Apaches throughout Arizona Territory. Various local newspapers provide numerous examples of extreme forms of enmity for Apaches who killed white citizens. Although the Apache wars had ended, a period of intense racial animosity toward Apaches permeated white society and continued for decades.[30]

FINAL OBSERVATIONS

How do we explain the treatment received by these Apache defendants within the Arizona Territory's nineteenth-century criminal justice system? In a 1980 dissenting opinion during the court of appeals hearing into Elmer "Geronimo" Pratt's murder conviction, Justice George William Dunn suggested, "A trial which is not fundamentally fair is no trial at all. It is a non sequitur to argue that a defendant is obviously guilty if it is an established fact that the defendant was not afforded a fair trial."[31] These Apache defendants, who could not understand the language in which their trials were conducted, were at great risk in the Arizona criminal justice system. They were unaware of their legal rights, and if law enforcement, judges, and prosecutors fail to protect all of an individual's rights, it is impossible for that person to receive a fair trial. Did the criminal justice system treat these Apache defendants fairly and protect all of their legal rights? Unfortunately, it did not. There are similar patterns of failure to provide fair legal treatment of indigenous populations in Canada, Australia, and New Zealand. Sidney Harring provides some striking examples that include multiple trials of Cree held in a single day. Furthermore, all-white juries returned guilty verdicts that showed little concern about the evidence presented against the Cree defendants. Peter Karsten offers examples of indiscriminate killing of Maoris in New Zealand land disputes, noting that in some cases they were "shot like dogs" by the white settlers squatting on Maori land.[32] Obviously, the Apaches were not the only ones suffering under a white-dominated legal system.

A variety of factors helps to illuminate the unfairness of a system that created this legal imbalance. Beginning with a criminal justice system that favored the white majority who controlled it. Sheriffs, jury members, attorneys, and judges came mainly from white society; consequently, Apache defendants were at a decided disadvantage throughout the legal process.

Second, if an individual could afford good legal counsel, his or her chances of acquittal were high; however, if a defendant was indigent, the results could be disastrous. The Apache defendants often received poor legal advice from their court-appointed attorneys, who may have been unaware that their actions frustrated the assumed fairness of the judicial system.

The third factor, three of these trials were remarkably short, was actually typical for Apache defendants. The trial transcripts for Captain Jack, Nahdeizaz, Gonshayee, and Batdish, the Apache defendants in this study, were 46, 24, 26, and 158 pages respectively. Three of the cases required less than a day, one actually just one half a day. It really is hard to believe that at a capital murder trial the jury could be impaneled, opening statements presented, testimony concluded, final arguments made by counsel, judge's instructions given, jury deliberations completed, and a guilty verdict reached in less than one day. But that is exactly what happened in three of these cases, and the fourth required less than three days. There is little doubt that these defendants received an inferior defense.

Fourth, nonwhite defendants, by their very nature, were confronted with a formidable barrier that prevented many of them from being treated fairly. The dominant society perceived Apache defendants as marginal people. They not only looked and dressed differently, but also spoke a variety of languages that sharply separated them from white society. Since most people have a tendency to judge others by their looks, one can only imagine how some white observers evaluated Gonshayee on his first appearance in the Pinal County courtroom. The photograph of Gonshayee and his fellow defendants suggests

further visual evidence about first impressions by jurors, prosecutors, and judges upon seeing him and the others for the first
time.[33]

As was detailed in the case studies, the Apache defendants
could not clearly understand the language in which the trials
were conducted and, because of faulty translation, were at risk
in the Arizona territorial criminal justice system. They could
neither understand their rights and the charges against them,
nor could they adequately state their cases when called to testify.

Finally, the killing of white members of society by an
Apache struck at the very nature of the right to be secure in
one's home in a civilized society. This kind of crime created fear
in the hearts and minds of white citizens, and members of the
criminal justice system had to address those concerns. It is clear
that the race of the victim was important to both jury and
judge, as well as to the public. By their actions, the prosecution,
judge, and jury were sending a strong message that nonwhites
would be harshly punished, especially if they selected and killed
white victims.[34]

To finish, we must return to Apache Kid, who was indicted by
Gila County authorities, sentenced to Yuma Prison, escaped, and
became the "renegade of renegades." After his conviction in Gila
County in 1889, he was being transported to the Yuma Territorial Prison to serve his sentence. During the slow, overland trip by
wagon the Kid and his fellow convicts overpowered and killed
the sheriff and escaped from custody. Three years later, on September 4, 1892, a story in the New York Times reported that
Apache Kid and his gang of "predatory Apaches" had been
causing trouble in the Arizona Territory and were allegedly ter-
rorizing white settlers. Although he actually had no gang, it made
for inflammatory rhetoric that sold newspapers. Not to mention,
one Apache "renegade" could not be causing all of this terroriza-

tion of the white population in Arizona Territory. Two months later a reporter noted that "the notorious Apache renegade" had once again evaded law enforcement officers, who were believed to have been hot on his trail.[35] Such front-page stories, of course, encouraged nineteenth-century whites to develop and maintain distorted images of Native Americans and help to explain how and why the white-dominated society treated Apache defendants accused of crimes as they did. In the historical literature of Native American culture compiled by contemporary white authors, Apaches were characterized as the most vicious and fiendish of all. Anglo Americans viewed Native Americans as impediments to civilization who needed to be removed at all costs and destroyed if necessary. Arizona residents perceived Apaches as vicious, ruthless, and ready to kill any unsuspecting whites. Many whites determined that extermination was the preferred method to deal with Apaches. Under such circumstance, it should not be surprising that these Apache defendants suffered under Arizona's criminal justice system.

NOTES

PROLOGUE

1. As quoted in an editorial essay by Charles L. Lindner, "A Study of Diverging Careers in the Geronimo Pratt Case," *Los Angeles Times*, February 28, 1999.

2. Powers, *Crime and Punishment*, 289–90, 302.

3. Kawashima, *Puritan Justice*, 149–50.

4. Ibid., 152–54.

5. Ibid., 164.

6. Ibid., 280.

7. Ibid., 176–78.

8. Harring, *White Man's Law*, 112–13; see also Hamar Foster, "Long-Distance Justice: The Criminal Justice Jurisdiction of Canadian Courts West of the Canadas, 1763–1859," *American Journal of Legal History* 34 (January 1990): 1–48.

9. Harring, *White Man's Law*, 113–15.

10. Ibid., 221–23.

11. Trials of Indian defendants often lasted less than a day. See McKanna, *Race and Homicide*, 1–2, 20–21.

12. Harring, *White Man's Law*, 231–34.

13. Ibid., 238.

186   NOTES

14. Ibid., 239, 241. Harring notes that few of them had legal training.

15. Ibid., 245–49.

16. Ibid., 249–50.

17. Ibid., 270–71.

18. Reece, *Aborigines and Colonist*, 149, 225–26. These early deaths follow similar patterns discovered in California; see McKanna, *Race and Homicide*, 100; see also Karsten, *Between Law and Custom*, 112–14.

19. Chomsky, "United States–Dakota War Trials," 17. When Myrick's dead body was discovered, his brother "knew precisely why his . . . mouth was stuffed with grass"; see also Ralph K. Andrist, *The Long Death: The Last Days of the Plains Indians* (New York: Collier Books, 1964), 56.

20. Chomsky, "United States–Dakota War Trials," 17.

21. Ibid., 21. Sibley, a colonel at the outbreak of the Dakota war, received a promotion to general.

22. Bessler, *Legacy of Violence*, 43.

23. Meyer, *History of the Santee Sioux*, 126.

24. Chomsky, "United States–Dakota War Trials," 25.

25. Ibid., 26.

26. Meyer, *History of the Santee Sioux*, 124.

27. Chomsky, "United States–Dakota War Trials," 24. The tribunal members were William R. Marshall and William Crooks, both colonels, captains Hiram S. Bailey and Hiram P. Grant, and Lieutenant Rollin C. Olin.

28. Ibid., 55.

29. Ibid., 23.

30. Ibid., 53.

31. Ibid., 27, 47; and Meyer, *History of the Santee Sioux*, 127.

32. Bessler, *Legacy of Violence*, 40.

33. Ibid., 54.

34. Ibid., 57–58.

35. Ibid., 61. After consulting with his aides, Lincoln had agreed to remove one of the condemned from the list.

36. Chomsky, "United States–Dakota War Trials," 27.

37. Ibid., 95.

38. Ibid., 38–39.

39. See McKanna, *Trial of "Indian Joe."*

40. See McKanna, *Race and Homicide,* 90–91, 98–99.

1. William Seagle, *Quest for Law* (New York: Alfred A. Knopf, 1941), 36.

2. Hoebel, *Law of Primitive Man,* 26.

3. Quoted in Hoebel, *Law of Primitive Man,* 26.

4. Ibid., 28 (emphasis in the original text).

5. Ibid., 158. For a discussion of Cheyenne criminal law, see Llewellyn and Hoebel, *Cheyenne Way,* 132–68.

6. Ibid., 159. The killing of an enemy tribesman was, of course, viewed in a different context. It was not only justifiable, but was encouraged by peer pressure and tribal tradition. For a discussion of homicide rates, see McKanna, *Homicide, Race, and Justice,* 155–63.

7. Reid, *Law of Blood,* 73, 100.

8. Ibid., 45, 101. See also John Phillip Reid, *Patterns of Vengeance: Crosscultural Homicide in the North American Fur Trade* (Ninth Judicial Circuit Historical Society, 1999).

9. Reid, *Law of Blood,* 139–41.

10. See Boyer, *Childhood and Folklore,* 30–32.

11. Goodwin, *Social Organization,* 393.

12. Stephen Wilson, *Feuding, Conflict and Banditry in Nineteenth-Century Corsica* (Cambridge: Harvard University Press, 1988); Jacob Black-Michaud, *Cohesive Force: Feud in the Mediterranean and the Middle East* (Oxford: Basil Blackwell, 1975); Christopher Boehm, *Blood Revenge: The Anthropology of Feuding in Montenegro and Other Tribal Societies* (Lawrence: University Press of Kansas, 1984); and Franco Ferracuti, Renato Lazzari, and Marvin E. Wolfgang, eds., *Violence in Sardinia* (Rome: Mario Bulzoni, Editore, 1970).

13. Goodwin, *Social Organization,* 398. The exact nature of tiswin is not clear. An alcoholic beverage made from corn, it is commonly called *tulapai* or *tulabai* by the Apaches. See James L. Haley,

Apaches: A History and Culture Portrait (Garden City, NY: Doubleday, 1981), 98.

14. Captain John L. Bullis, acting U.S. Indian agent to the commissioner of Indian Affairs, August 26, 1889, in *Annual Report of the Commissioner of Indian Affairs, 1889,* 122.

15. Goodwin, *Social Organization,* 402, 404. The retaliation could come quickly or many months later, when the killer least expected it.

16. Ibid., 406. This was an exceptional case, but it indicates that retaliation in such feuds could be explosive.

17. Ibid., 408–9.

18. Opler, *Apache Life-Way,* 459.

19. Goodwin, *Social Organization,* 395–96.

20. Ibid., 397–98.

21. Ibid., 399.

22. Lockwood, *Apache Indians,* 44.

23. Goodwin's *Social Organization* provides the best appraisal of Apache custom, particularly chapter seven, "Social Adjustments," 374–427; see also Opler, *Apache Life-Way,* 140–85, 336–53, 406–14; Cremony, *Life Among the Apaches,* 87–90, 285–97; and Bourke, "Medicine-Men of the Apache."

24. Goodwin, *Social Organization,* 189–90.

25. Ibid., 190.

26. Clum, *Apache Agent,* 34.

27. Ibid., 97.

28. Ibid., 98.

29. Ibid., 187–95. Tahzay, the son of Cochise, died of pneumonia in Washington, D.C.

30. Goodwin, *Western Apache Raiding,* 200–202. This may have been the beginning of the dispute between Captain Jack and Casadora.

31. Ibid., 316n.

32. Ibid., 182.

33. Goodwin, *Social Organization,* 32.

34. *U.S. v. Captain Jack,* testimony of Colonel Simon Snyder, 23.

35. Goodwin, *Western Apache Raiding,* 182.

36. *U.S. v. Captain Jack,* testimony of Casadora, 6.

37. See title 28, chap. 4, Government of Indian Country, secs. 2144 and 2146, in *Revised Statutes, 1873–1874,* 376.

38. See title 70, sec. 5339, in *Revised Statutes, 1873–1874,* 18, pt. 1, 1038; and sec. 273, in *Statutes at Large, 1907–1909,* 35, pt. 1, 1143. Congress divided homicide into first- and second-degree in 1909.

39. See chap. 341, in *Statutes at Large, 1883–1885,* 363–85; and *U.S. v. Kagama,* 118 U.S. 375–85 (1886). This legal change occurred as a result of *Ex Parte Crow Dog* 109 U.S. 556–72 (1883). The U.S. Supreme Court overturned a murder conviction of Crow Dog, creating a great uproar. With intense pressure from white citizens, Congress passed the Major Crimes Act in 1885 as a part of the general Indian Appropriations bill.

40. Gorton Carruth and Eugene Ehrlich, *Harper Book of American Quotes* (New York: Harper and Row, 1988), 307. Comment made in a speech he gave in Washington, D.C., October 22, 1883.

41. Oliver Wendell Holmes, "Law in Science and Science in Law," *Harvard Law Review* 12 (1899): 237–38.

42. Philip Francis, *How to Serve on a Jury* (New York: Oceana Publications, 1953), 17.

43. Mark Twain, *Roughing It* (New York: P. F. Collier and Son, 1913), 57.

44. See Bakken, *Practicing Law,* 99–113

45. McKanna, *Race and Homicide,* 29–30, 49–50, 71, 94–95.

46. McKanna, "Life Hangs in the Balance," 208–9.

47. One historian claimed that since Indians were indigent, the court had to appoint attorneys to defend them. They "were paid a fee of $50 for each case. . . . Scores of attorneys flocked to . . . get this practice." See Hayes, *Apache Vengeance,* 54.

48. Demurrer filed by H. N. Alexander and L. H. Chalmers, May 19, 1888, in *U.S. v. Captain Jack.*

49. Ibid.

50. Ibid., jury role. The jury consisted of F. Franklin, F. M. Griffin, Charles Banker, C. F. Palmer, J. W. Copes, E. B. Kirkland, Peter Will,

M. M. Hickey, T. H. Bramrick, William Miller, Charles A. Boake, and M. G. Hill. The jury selected Boake as its foreman.

51. Goodwin, *Western Apache Raiding*, 183.

52. Ibid., 184.

53. *U.S. v. Captain Jack*, testimony of Casadora, 1. The SI band members included Ztalnaki, Luchua, Guda, Gagol, Taguchua, Dastha, Nasua, and Nachona.

54. Ibid., 2–5.

55. Ibid., 9.

56. Ibid., 7.

57. Ibid., 10.

58. Ibid., testimony of Ztalnaki, 11.

59. Ibid., 12. Since they were at least fifty to sixty yards from the shooters, they could not have heard what they said unless they hollered loudly.

60. Ibid., 13.

61. Ibid., testimony of Gagol, 15–16.

62. Ibid., 17.

63. Ibid., testimony of Captain P. L. Lee, 18.

64. Ibid., 19.

65. Ibid., 20–21.

66. Ibid., testimony of Colonel Simon Snyder, 22–23.

67. Ibid., 24.

68. Ibid.

69. Ibid., testimony of Captain Jack, 26.

70. Ibid., 27.

71. Ibid., testimony of Casadora, 6.

72. Ibid., testimony of Captain Jack, 28.

73. Ibid., 28–29.

74. Ibid., 29.

75. Ibid., testimony of Colonel Snyder, 23–24.

76. Ibid., 24.

77. Ibid., testimony of Tillychillay, 31.

78. Ibid., 30.

79. Ibid., 31–32.

80. Ibid., testimony of Hastindutody, 32–33.

81. Ibid., 34.

82. Ibid., testimony of Ilthkah, 40.

83. Ibid., 38–39.

84. Ibid., 39.

85. Ibid., testimony of Tzayzintilth, 41.

86. Ibid., testimony of Lahcohn, 44.

87. Ibid., testimony of Lieutenant Watson, 35.

88. Ibid., 37.

89. Ibid., motion to the court by H. N. Alexander, 45.

90. Ibid., counter argument by Baker, 45.

91. Ibid., second motion to the court by Alexander, 46.

92. Ibid., ruling by U.S. District Court Judge William W. Porter, 46.

93. Ibid., verdict of the jury, May 22, 1888.

94. Ibid., arrest of judgment, filed June 5, 1888.

95. Friedman and Percival, *Roots of Justice,* 185. Trials of short duration, however, were common for Indian defendants during the nineteenth century. There is little doubt that these other cases also received an inferior defense. Sidney Harring discovered similarly short transcripts involving Native Americans accused of murder. One case file involving Machekequonabe, a Canadian Cree, contained a "twelve-page official transcript." See Sidney Harring, *White Man's Law,* 389; *U.S. v. Nahdeizaz,* 1887; *U.S. v. Gonshayee,* 1888; and *Territory of Arizona v. Batdish,* 1890. In his research on law practiced on the California frontier, Gordon Bakken discovered that "trials lengthened" by 1885. One particular trial had been in court for "4 or 5 days." Bakken, *Practicing Law,* 111.

96. Prisoner delivery by U.S. Marshal W. K. Meade, *U.S. v. Captain Jack.*

97. Register of Prisoners and Index, Ohio State Penitentiary, 355–56, Ohio State Historical Society.

98. Application of Captain Jack for a writ of habeas corpus, in the Supreme Court of the United States, *Ex Parte: In the Matter of Captain Jack,* no. 8, October Term, 1888 (Washington, D.C.: National Archives) and chap. 341, sec. 9, Major Crimes Act, Indian Appropriations Act, March 3, 1885, in *Statutes at Large, 1883–1885,* 385.

99. Ibid., 2.

100. Ibid.

101. Ibid.

102. *Ex Parte Captain Jack*, 130 U.S. 354 (1889).

103. Ilthkah had died in the Ohio State prison while awaiting the court appeal.

104. Verdict of the jury, Arizona Territorial Court, October 28, 1889, in *Territory of Arizona v. Captain Jack*.

105. Sidney Harring discovered similar results involving murder trials of Cree in Saskatchewan, Canada. See Harring, *White Man's Law*, 221, 239–50. For a discussion of treatment of indigenous populations in Australia, Canada, and New Zealand, see Karsten, *Between Law and Custom*, 107–18; and Lauren Benton, *Law and Colonial Cultures: Legal Regimes in World History, 1400–1900* (London: Cambridge University Press, 2002), 86–102.

106. See title 28, chap. 4, Government of Indian Country, secs. 2144 and 2146, in *Revised Statutes, 1873–1874*, 376.

CHAPTER 2

1. *Ulzana's Raid*, Universal Pictures, 1972. The film, directed by Robert Aldrich, stars Burt Lancaster, Bruce Davison, and Richard Jaeckel.

2. Ulzana's real name is shrouded in mystery. Dan Thrapp claims that his name was Josanie and that he was the brother of Chihuahua. Paul I. Wellman calls him Ulzana, whereas Eve Ball uses both names. See Thrapp, *Conquest of Apacheria*, 334–39; Wellman, *Death in the Desert*, 241–47; and Ball, *Indeh*, 45, 50, 99.

3. Wellman, *Death in the Desert*, 241–47; Thrapp, *Conquest of Apacheria*, 334–39; Ball, *Indeh*, 45, 50, 99; and John Upton Terrell, *Apache Chronicle* (New York: World Publishing, 1972), 374–81.

4. Opler, *Apache Life-Way*, 369–70.

5. Ibid. and Aleš Hrdlička, "Method of Preparing Treavino Among the White River Apaches," *American Anthropologist* (n.s.) 6 (1904): 191.

6. Bourke, "Distillation," 297.

7. Frederick Lloyd, acting assistant surgeon, U.S.A, *Special Re-*

port on Indians at San Carlos Agency, Arizona (San Carlos Agency, 1883), 6.

8. See particularly Report of San Carlos Agency, Captain F. E. Pierce, acting agent, *Report of the Commissioner of Indian Affairs, 1886*, 40; and Report of San Carlos Agency, Brevet Lieutenant-Colonel Lewis Johnson, *Report of the Commissioner of Indian Affairs, 1893*, 122.

9. Report of San Carlos Agency, J. C. Tiffany, Indian agent, *Annual Report of the Commissioner of Indian Affairs to the Secretary of the Interior for the Year 1881*, 9, 11.

10. Report of San Carlos Agency, Captain John L. Bullis, *Fifty-Eighth Annual Report of the Commissioner of Indian Affairs to the Secretary of the Interior, 1889*, 122.

11. Report of San Carlos Agency, George D. Corson, Indian agent, *Annual Report of the Commissioner of Indian Affairs to the Secretary of the Interior, 1901*, 121.

12. Davis, *Truth about Geronimo*, 145–46; and Thrapp, *Conquest of Apacheria*, 211–16.

13. Davis, *Truth about Geronimo*, 145.

14. See Thrapp, *Al Sieber*, 322; William Sparks, *The Apache Kid: A Bear Fight and Other True Stories of the Old West* (Los Angeles: Skelton, 1926), 10–15; and testimony of Sayes, June 1, 1888, in *U.S. v. Say-es*, U.S. District Court, Second Judicial District, Territory of Arizona, 13. The many versions of his Apache name include Skibenanted, Oskabennantelz, Ohyessonna, Gjonteee, Zenogolache, Shisininty, Haskaybaynayntal, and Eskibinadel.

15. Thrapp, *Al Sieber*, 323.

16. Dan R. Williamson, "Al Sieber, Famous Scout of the Southwest," *Arizona Historical Review* 3 (January 1931): 67; and Wharfield, "Footnotes to History," 39.

17. See title 28, chap. 4, Government of Indian Country, secs. 2144 and 2146, in *Revised Statute, 1873-1874*, 376; and Wharfield, "Footnotes to History," 40.

18. General Court Martial of First Sergeant Kid, testimony of Captain F. E. Pierce, 36–37.

19. Ibid., testimony of Kid, 116; and testimony of Bachoandoth, in

Report of Appeals in the Court Martial of First Sergeant Kid at San Carlos, to W. C. Endicott, secretary of war from judge advocate general's office, April 11, 1888, 42.

20. General Court Martial of First Sergeant Kid, testimony of Kid, 116.

21. Ibid., testimony of Captain F. E. Pierce, 36–37.

22. Opler, *Apache Life-Way,* 332–33, 342.

23. See Boyer, *Childhood and Folklore,* 30–32.

24. General Court Martial of First Sergeant Kid, testimony of Pierce, 51.

25. *Arizona Weekly Citizen,* June 11, 1887; and Reports of General Nelson A. Miles, Renegade Indians, June 1887–May 1889, *Letters Received by the Office of the Adjutant General,* Main Series, 1881–1889, National Archives; dispatch from M. Barber, A. A. General, to Fort Grant, Arizona Territory, June 3, 1887.

26. Opler, *Apache Life-Way,* 347.

27. U.S. District Court, Second District, Arizona Territory, see mittimus pending examination, December 28, 1888. Authorities indicted Apache Kid for the killing of Michael Grace on or about June 15, 1887.

28. Reports of General Miles, Renegade Indians, dispatch from Major General O. O. Howard to adjutant general of the Army, June 9, 1887.

29. *Arizona Weekly Citizen,* June 11, 1887.

30. Reports of General Miles, Renegade Indians, dispatch from General Howard to adjutant general of the Army, June 15, 1887.

31. Ibid., dispatch from General Miles to Captain Pierce, San Carlos, June 11, 1887.

32. Ibid., dispatch from General Miles to commanding officers in the field, June 15, 1887, and dispatch from General Howard to adjutant general of the Army, June 15, 1887.

33. Ibid., dispatch from General Miles to Lieutenant Johnson, June 18, 1887.

34. Ibid., dispatch from General Miles to assistant adjutant general, June 25, 1887.

35. Annual Report of Brigadier General Nelson A. Miles, commanding Department of Arizona, September 3, 1887, p. 4.

36. General Court Martial of First Sergeant Kid, Company A, Indian Scouts, Judge Advocate General, Records Received, 4475, December 27, 1887 (Washington D.C.: National Archives), 17–18, 36–37.

37. Ibid., testimony of Captain F. E. Pierce, 36–37.

38. Ibid., comments by judge advocate, 41.

39. Ibid., testimony of Pierce, 41–44.

40. Ibid., testimony of Pierce, 46.

41. Ibid., testimony of Pierce, 47–48.

42. Ibid., testimony of Al Sieber, 55–56.

43. Ibid., testimony of Sieber, 58–59.

44. Ibid., testimony of Antonio Díaz, 89.

45. Ibid., testimony of Díaz, 92.

46. Ibid., testimony of Díaz, 96.

47. Ibid., testimony of Sieber, 99–104.

48. Ibid., testimony of Gonshayee, 105–7.

49. Ibid., testimony of Sayes, 109–12.

50. Ibid., testimony of First Sergeant Kid, 115–16.

51. Ibid., testimony of Kid, 117–18.

52. Ibid., testimony of Pierce, 50.

53. Ibid., summation for the defense by Lieutenant James Baldwin, 118.

54. Ibid., summation by Baldwin, 120.

55. Ibid., summation by Baldwin, 121–24.

56. Ibid., summation by Baldwin, 124.

57. Ibid., summation by Baldwin, 127–28.

58. Ibid., sentence of the court-martial panel, signed by Major Anson Mills, 130–31.

59. *U.S. v. Gonshayee*, demurrer filed by H. N. Alexander and L. H. Chalmers, May 29, 1888.

60. Ibid., testimony of John Scanlan, 3–5.

61. Ibid., question by Judge William W. Porter, 13.

62. Ibid., testimony of Vacasheviejo, 14–16.

63. Ibid., testimony of Vacasheviejo, 17.

64. Ibid., testimony of Vacasheviejo, 17.

65. Ibid., testimony of Vacasheviejo, 19.

66. Ibid., testimony of Bashlalah, 21–22.

67. Ibid., testimony of Sayes, 23.

68. Ibid., testimony of Antonio Díaz, 24.

69. Ibid., statement to the Judge by H. N. Alexander, counsel for defense, 25.

70. Ibid., verdict presented by jury foreman Charles A. Boake, June 4, 1888. The other jurors were John Hickey, H. B. St. Clair, E. G. Wheeler, George F. Coats, T. A. Cochrone, B. Cory, C. J. Dyer, W. F. McNunty, A. A. Utley, A. E. Cobb, and W. A. Hall.

71. On trial length, see Harring, *White Man's Law*, 221, 231. In an examination of the treatment of Native Americans in Canada, Harring discovered that "in legal terms, the quality of justice rendered was a travesty." Ibid., 247.

72. *U.S. v. Gonshayee*, motion in arrest of judgment filed June 14, 1888, for the defendant by H. N. Alexander and L. H. Chalmers.

73. Ibid., sentence of U.S. District Court Judge William W. Porter, filed June 14, 1888.

74. Ibid., notice of appeal filed for Gonshayee in the Supreme Court of the Territory of Arizona, June 14, 1888.

75. Hayes, *Apache Vengeance*, 54.

76. Chap. 341, sec. 9, Major Crimes Act, Indian Appropriations Act, March 3, 1885, in *Statutes at Large, 1883–1885*, 385.

77. *U.S. v. Kagama*, 118 U.S. 383–84 (1886); see Newton, "Federal Power over Indians," 212–18.

78. *U.S. v. Kagama*, 118 U.S. 385 (1886).

79. Federal law dealing with homicide only recognized first-degree murder, which called for the death penalty. See sec. 5339 in *Revised Statute, 1873–74*, 18, pt. 1, 1038. One can understand, then, why the Supreme Court justice suggested that the defendant was entitled to the same trial as others in the various county jurisdictions that recognized first- and second-degree murder.

80. *Ex Parte Gonshayee* 130 U.S. 344 (1889), Case 49 in Arizona Supreme Court, Territorial Records.

81. See *Ex Parte Crow Dog* 109 U.S. 556 (1883) and chap. 341, sec. 9, Major Crimes Act, 385.

82. See sec. 5339 in *Revised Statute, 1873–74*, 18, pt. 1, 1038.

83. *Ex Parte Gonshayee* 130 U.S. 353 (1889).

84. The other defendants were Nahconquisay, Eskahkilla, Muelgasla, Kohdasla, Pahslagosla, Gonahtan, and Askisaylala. See Pinal County District Court case files 15, 24, and 35, October 1889, Arizona State Archives.

85. *Arizona Weekly Enterprise*, October 19, 1889.

86. Ibid.

87. *Arizona Champion*, October 26, 1889.

88. *Arizona Weekly Enterprise*, November 16, 1889. In Canada, Sidney Harring discovered a similar policy: "The crown intended to stage these trials with the intent of breaking the back of Indian resistance to the federal government's Indian policy." All-white juries "returned 'guilty' verdicts no matter what the evidence." Harring, *White Man's Law*, 247.

CHAPTER 3

1. Thomas G. Tousey, *Military History of Carlisle and Carlisle Barracks* (Richmond, Va.: Dietz Press, 1939), 285–86.

2. Fear-Segal, "Nineteenth-Century Indian Education," 328.

3. Chapman, "Little Red Indian School," 48–50.

4. Ibid., 52.

5. Ibid., 53.

6. Pratt, *Battlefield and Classroom*, 246–47.

7. Ibid., 237–38; and Eastman, *Pratt*, 206.

8. Eastman, *Pratt*, 209.

9. Ibid., 233.

10. Fear-Segal, "Nineteenth-Century Indian Education," 339.

11. Report of Richard Henry Pratt to the secretary of the interior, October 5, 1880, *Annual Report of the Secretary of the Interior, 1880*, 301.

12. Ibid., September 12, 1884, *Annual Report of the Secretary of the Interior, 1884*, 188.

13. Ibid., September 7, 1887, *Annual Report of the Commissioner of Indian Affairs to the Secretary of the Interior, 1887*, 256–57.

14. Ibid., August 17, 1888, *Annual Report of the Commissioner of Indian Affairs to the Secretary of the Interior, 1888*, 278.

15. Ball, *Indeh*, 149.

16. Report of Richard Henry Pratt to the secretary of the interior, September 1, 1889, *Annual Report of the Commissioner of Indian Affairs to the Secretary of the Interior, 1889*, 367.

17. Stockel, *Survival of the Spirit*, 125.

18. Ibid. The actual number of Apaches that died of disease at Carlisle remains unknown. There were at least fifty-six Apache children who perished; however, this number does not include the many Apaches who were sent home to die. See Stockel, *Survival of the Spirit*, 131–36.

19. Betzinez, *I Fought with Geronimo*, 149.

20. Chapman, "Little Red Indian School," 50–51. The young Apaches were provided with matching uniforms and dresses.

21. Ball, *Indeh*, 144. After Eve Ball interviewed Daklugie, she observed that "it took four years to get him to talk." His experience at Carlisle had been less than satisfactory and he held strong feelings about whites inquiring about his life there. Ibid., xiii. See also Greenfeld, "Escape from Albuquerque," 47–71.

22. Betzinez, *I Fought with Geronimo*, 153, 156.

23. Coleman, *American Indian Children*, 180.

24. Ibid., 183.

25. Ibid., 188–89.

26. P. P. Wilcox, to Indian commissioner, August 15, 1884, *Annual Report of the Commissioner of Indian Affairs to the Secretary of the Interior, 1884*, 9.

27. Testimony of Captain F. E. Pierce, acting Indian agent, San Carlos Agency, October 20, 1885. *Report of Committees of the House of Representatives, 1885–1886*, 132.

28. Meriam, *Problem of Indian Administration*, 407.

29. Bender, *Study of Western Apache*, 114–15, 127.

30. Braatz, *Surviving Conquest*, 195–203.

31. Bender, *Study of Western Apache*, 136.

32. Report of J. C. Tiffany, Indian agent, August 15, 1880, *Annual Report of the Commissioner of Indian Affairs to the Secretary of the Interior, 1880,* 6.

33. *Annual Report of the Commissioner of Indian Affairs to the Secretary of the Interior, 1880,* xxi–xxii.

34. Report of Tiffany, August 15, 1880, ibid., 6.

35. Report of Tiffany, September 6, 1881, ibid., 7–8.

36. Ibid., 9–11.

37. Captain F. E. Pierce, August 31, 1886, *Annual Report of the Commissioner of Indian Affairs to the Secretary of the Interior, 1886,* 40.

38. Captain John L. Bullis, acting agent, August 24, 1888, *Fifty-Seventh Annual Report of the Commissioner of Indian Affairs to the Secretary of the Interior, 1888,* 7.

39. *Arizona Weekly Citizen,* March 26, 1887.

40. Ball, *Indeh,* 37.

41. Mott, ranked 114th in his class at West Point, received an appointment to Adjutant Commanding Company "A" Indian Scouts effective December 21, 1886. See *Letters Received by the Office of the Adjutant General,* Main Series, 1881–1889, in Reports of General Nelson A. Miles, Commander at San Carlos Reservation, National Archives; *Official Register of the U.S. Containing a List of Officers and Employees in the Civil, Military, and Naval Service on the First of July, 1885,* vol. 1 (Washington, D.C.: Government Printing Office, 1885), 399, 436; and Dan L. Thrapp, *Encyclopedia of Frontier Biography,* vol. 2 (Glendale, Calif.: Arthur H. Clarke, 1988), 1027.

42. P. P. Wilcox, to Indian commissioner, August 15, 1884, *Annual Report of the Commissioner of Indian Affairs to the Secretary of the Interior, 1884,* 8.

43. *Annual Report of the Commissioner of Indian Affairs to the Secretary of the Interior, 1880,* xxi–xxii.

44. Wilcox, to Indian commissioner, August 15, 1884, in *Annual Report of the Commissioner of Indian Affairs to the Secretary of the Interior, 1884,* 8; and Braatz, *Surviving Conquest,* 188–89.

45. See Thrapp, *Al Sieber,* 319. In developing this account of the

dispute, Thrapp, unfortunately, relies too heavily upon Jess G. Hayes's untenable version, which is obviously flawed.

46. Ibid.

47. *U.S. v. Nahdeizaz,* testimony of Nahdeizaz, 15. From the testimony at the trial it is unclear what Lieutenant Mott said to Nahdeizaz. Frank Porter and Kayzay claimed that they did not hear Mott's rejoinder to Nahdeizaz; however, his reaction suggests that Mott threatened to jail him.

48. Ibid., 16. One secondary account erroneously claims that he only fired one shot at Mott. See Hayes, *Apache Vengeance,* 13. Dr. T. B. Davis, who examined the body, claimed that "he had three wounds. One in the arm, one in the thigh, and the third in the buttock, penetrating the pelvic cavity." He further testified that the latter wound, the deadly one, occurred while Mott was running from Nahdeizaz. *U.S. v. Nahdeizaz,* testimony of Nahdeizaz, 11–12.

49. See Ahearn, "Assimilationist Racism," 23–32; Ronald M. Johnson, "Schooling the Savage: Andrew S. Draper and Indian Education," *Phylon* 35 (March 1974): 74–82; Rubenstein, "To Destroy a Culture," 151–60; and Robert H. Keller Jr., "American Indian Education: An Historical Context," *Journal of the West* 13 (April 1974): 75–82.

50. See *U.S. v. Nahdeizaz,* verdict of the jury, 24; and Prison Registers, 1887, Arizona Prison, RG 85.

51. *U.S. v. Nahdeizaz,* indictment for murder, May 9, 1887.

52. Ibid., demurrer filed by A. D. Duff and E. J. Edwards, May 10, 1887.

53. Ibid., demurrer filed by Duff and Edwards, May 11, 1887. The demurrer further complained that the "indictment does not substantially conform to the requirements of secs. 213 and 214 of chap. 11, compiled laws of Arizona."

54. *U.S. v. Nahdeizaz,* jury role. The attorneys accepted P. H. Coyle, W. T. Woods Jr., G. W. Brooks, John G. Wheeler, J. P. Patkinson, H. A. Wilson, T. A. Cockran, J. M. Gregory, J. M. Schriver, E. G. Wheeler, G. W. Coble, and M. H. Sherman for the jury.

55. This, of course, was not the only short trial of an Indian defendant; Sidney Harring discovered similar trials involving Indians that

often "took only a few hours," and, in other cases, they "consumed all of one day." Harring, *White Man's Law*, 221, 231. In the American West, however, this was, indeed, a short trial; in nineteenth-century Alameda County, the average homicide trial lasted seven days. See Friedman and Percival, *Roots of Justice*, 185.

56. *U.S. v. Nahdeizaz*, testimony of Frank T. Porter, 2–3.
57. Ibid., testimony of Porter, 2–3.
58. Ibid., testimony of Porter, 3–4.
59. Ibid., testimony of Porter, 4.
60. *Arizona Weekly Citizen*, March 26, 1887.
61. *U.S. v. Nahdeizaz*, testimony of Porter, 6.
62. Ibid., testimony of Porter, 7.
63. Ibid., testimony of Porter, 8.
64. Ibid., testimony of Porter, 9.
65. Ibid., testimony of Porter, 10.
66. Ibid., testimony of Dr. T. B. Davis, 11.
67. Ibid., testimony of Davis, 12.
68. Ibid., testimony of Davis, 12–13.
69. Ibid., order of the court, 14.
70. Ibid., testimony of Nahdeizaz, 14.
71. Ibid., testimony of Nahdeizaz, 14.
72. Ibid., testimony of Nahdeizaz, 15.
73. Ibid., testimony of Nahdeizaz, 15.
74. Ibid., testimony of Nahdeizaz, 16.
75. Ibid., testimony of Kayzay, 17.
76. Ibid., testimony of Kayzay, 18.
77. Ibid., instructions of Judge William W. Porter, 21.
78. Ibid., instructions of Porter, 23.
79. Ibid., verdict of the jury, 24.
80. *Territory of Arizona v. Nahdeizaz*, Case no. 113, District Court, Second Judicial District, Gila County, October 23, 1889, indictment for murder. The prosecution called Frank Porter, Juan Butcher, and Dr. T. B. Davis to testify before the grand jury.
81. Ibid.
82. Hayes, *Apache Vengeance*, 59.
83. Ibid., 60.

84. Thrapp, *Al Sieber,* 337.

85. Utley, "Ordeal of Plenty Horses," 17.

86. Ibid., 86.

87. Ibid., 84.

88. Ibid.

CHAPTER 4

1. *Territory of Arizona v. Batdish, Bakelcle, Guadalupe, and Natsin,* 4–10.

2. Ibid., testimony of Edward B. Ingalls, 26.

3. Ibid., testimony of George Shute, 29–32.

4. Federal Bureau of Investigation, *The Identification Division of the FBI* (Washington, D.C.: U.S. Department of Justice, 1991), 2.

5. Mark Twain, *Pudd'nhead Wilson* (1894; repr., Mineola, N.Y.: Dover Publications, 1999), 115.

6. Taylor, *Principles and Practice;* and Taylor, *Manual of Medical Jurisprudence;* see Morland, *Outline of Scientific Criminology,* 109.

7. Allan McL. Hamilton, "The Scientific Detection of Crime," *Appletons' Journal of Literature, Science, and Art* 15 (June 24, 1876): 826.

8. Melville Davisson Post, *The Man Hunters* (New York: J. H. Sears, 1926), 291–301; and A. Lucas, *Forensic Chemistry and Scientific Investigation* (New York: Longmans, Green, 1935), 187.

9. Moriarity, "Cast of Footprints," 229–32.

10. *People v. E. P. McCurdy,* 68 Cal 582–83 (1886).

11. *People v. C. W. Myers,* 70 Cal 583 (1886).

12. Schmitt, *General George Crook,* 181.

13. Ibid., 182.

14. Robinson, *Diaries of John Gregory Bourke,* 34.

15. Ibid., 37.

16. Ibid., 62.

17. Ibid., 82.

18. Smith, *View from Officers' Row,* 165–66, 168.

19. Ibid., 169.

20. Ibid., 170.

21. Ibid., 171, 173.

22. John G. Bourke, *On the Border with Crook* (Lincoln: University of Nebraska Press, 1971), 203.

23. Ibid., 247–59.

24. Detachment of Indian Scouts, July 19, 1892, San Carlos Agency, Arizona Historical Society.

25. Wharfield, *Apache Indian Scouts*, 71.

26. Ibid., 73.

27. Ibid., 76.

28. Ibid., 76–77.

29. Ibid., 78.

30. Ibid., 79, 81–82.

31. Smith, *View from Officers' Row*, 171.

32. Tate, "'Pershing's Pets,'" 57–58.

33. Ibid., 61–63.

34. Ibid., 67–69.

35. *Territory of Arizona v. Batdish, Bakelcle, Guadalupe, and Natsin,* testimony of Al Sieber, 78–80.

36. Ibid., testimony of Sieber, 81. It is worth noting that both Massai and Apache Kid were known to seize women and young girls during their periodic raids on San Carlos camps. In 1886, Geronimo surrendered, and during the removal of the Chiricahua Apaches to Florida, Massai jumped off a train and returned to Arizona, where he took his revenge against whites and Apaches. This incident strongly suggests that Massai committed this killing.

37. Ibid., testimony of Guadalupe, 120–21.

38. Ibid., 1–2.

39. Ibid., testimony of J. H. Baker, 4–7.

40. Ibid., testimony of Baker, 8–10.

41. Ibid., testimony of Baker, 15–16, 24. Baker provided conflicting testimony about the stolen horse. In one place he said it was unshod, but he also claimed that all of the horses used by the killers were shod.

42. Ibid., testimony of Edward B. Ingalls, 26.

43. Ibid., testimony of George Shute, 32.

44. Ibid., testimony of Knowles, 35.

45. Ibid., testimony of Knowles, 37.

46. Ibid., testimony of S. S. Patterson, 45.

47. Ibid., testimony of Patterson, 45.

48. Ibid., testimony of Patterson, 45–47.

49. Ibid., testimony of Patterson, 48–49.

50. Ibid., testimony of Patterson, 51.

51. Ibid., testimony of Patterson, 55–57.

52. Ibid., testimony of William H. Beard, 59.

53. Ibid., testimony of Beard, 60–61.

54. Ibid., testimony of Beard, 61–62.

55. Ibid., testimony of Al Sieber, 79–80.

56. Ibid., testimony of Sieber, 89–90.

57. Ibid., testimony of Sieber, 81. This testimony about the shooting of the women and a girl being stolen fits well with the methods employed by Massai, a "renegade."

58. Ibid., testimony of Sieber, 88–91.

59. Ibid., testimony of Jetanaki, 64–67.

60. Ibid., testimony of Jetanaki, 69.

61. Ibid., questions by Judge Joseph Kibbey, 75.

62. Ibid., testimony of John Daisy, 77.

63. Ibid., testimony of Richard Baker, 92–94.

64. For a discussion of the development of criminal law in California, see Bakken, *Practicing Law,* 104–11.

65. *Territory of Arizona v. Batdish, Bakelcle, Guadalupe, and Natsin,* testimony of Guadalupe, 118–19.

66. Ibid., 123.

67. Ibid., 124–26.

68. Ibid., testimony of Bakelcle, 129.

69. Ibid., 130–31.

70. Ibid., 135–36.

71. Ibid., testimony of Martin Gentry, 140–42.

72. Ibid., testimony of Guadalupe, 143.

73. Ibid., testimony of Batdish, 144–47.

74. Ibid., testimony of Natsin, 149–50.

75. Ibid., testimony of Lieutenant Jones, 152–53.

76. Ibid., J. D. McCabe, 153.

77. Ibid., testimony of Jones, 154.

78. Ibid., question by Judge Kibbey, 158.

79. *Territory of Arizona v. Batdish, Bakelcle, Natsin, and Guadalupe, 1891*, brief and argument, 3.

80. Ibid., 3.

81. Ibid., 4.

82. Ibid., 5.

83. Ibid., 6.

84. Ibid., 6–7.

85. Ibid., 7.

86. Ibid., 8.

87. Ibid., 9.

88. Ibid., 10–11.

89. Ibid., 11 (emphasis in the original text).

90. Ibid., 12.

91. Ibid.

92. Ibid., 14.

93. Ibid., 15.

94. Ibid., 17.

95. Ibid., 18–20

96. Ibid., 20.

97. Ibid., 20–21. In support of their argument, defense counsel cited *People v. Shuler*, 28 Cal 490 (1865); *People v. Strong*, 30 Cal 151 (1866); and *People v. Dick*, 32 Cal 213 (1867).

98. *Batdish, Bakelcle, Guadalupe, & Natsin, Appellant. v. The Territory of Arizona*, Appellee, in the Supreme Court of the Territory of Arizona, January 25, 1893, Case no. 67 (Phoenix: Arizona State Archives).

99. *People v. Shuler*, 28 Cal 495 (1865).

100. *People v. Strong*, 30 Cal 153–54 (1866).

101. *People v. Dick*, 32 Cal 213–16 (1867).

102. Quoted in Thrapp, *Al Sieber*, 347.

103. In Canada, Sidney Harring discovered that all-white juries returned guilty verdicts in cases involving Indian defendants "no matter what the evidence." Harring, *White Man's Law*, 247.

EPILOGUE

1. Sidney Harring notes that during the 1880s government officials in Battleford, Saskatchewan, Canada, refused to assign legal council for Cree Indian defendants and completed "a number of murder trials in one day." Harring, *White Man's Law,* 249. See also Friedman and Percival, *Roots of Justice,* 185.

2. See Hietter, "How Wild Was Arizona?" 183–210.

3. A survey of the U.S. District Court revealed that 81 percent of the fifty-eight murder cases were against Native Americans. Most of them involved Apache defendants from Apache, Gila, and Graham counties during the 1880s. These homicides usually occurred on or near the San Carlos Agency. See McKanna, "Life Hangs in the Balance," 208–9.

4. Hietter's study of Pima County confirms low conviction rates for whites, but fails to separate Indian defendants from his aggregate data. See Heitter, "How Wild Was Arizona?" 204–8. The U.S. District Court convictions follow a similar pattern, with 82 percent of the Native Americans being convicted. All U.S. District Court murder cases involving Native Americans as defendants occurred within one decade, 1882–1888. Thereafter, the Arizona territorial county courts handled virtually all of the cases involving homicide committed on or near reservations. McKanna, "Life Hangs in the Balance," 208–9.

5. See McKanna, *Race and Homicide,* 28–30. The Arizona data parallels similar statistics collected in seven California counties.

6. In a similar case in San Diego County, authorities encouraged Augustin Castro to plead guilty in order to avoid execution. His chances of acquittal or being found guilty on a lesser charge were good. Without good counsel, however, he suffered a long period of incarceration (thirty years) in San Quentin. See *People v. Augustin Castro* (1872), District Court, San Diego County (San Diego: San Diego Historical Society Archives).

7. See *The Territory of Arizona v. Chapaw, Eskaydapony, Tonikai, Nesho, Machukay, Bhasaduha, 1892–1897,* Criminal Case Files 178, 206, 241, 256, 268, and 280 in Registers of Criminal Action and Criminal Case Files, 1880–1920, RG 103.

8. See Registers of Criminal Action, RG 103.

9. See McKanna, "Murderers All," 359–69.

10. Seventy-three percent of these cases involved Apache male victims and usually included the use of tiswin. Registers of Criminal Action, RG 103.

11. *Arizona Silver Belt,* October 7, 1911.

12. Ibid.

13. See Stephen Wilson, *Feuding, Conflict, and Banditry in Nineteenth-Century Corsica* (Cambridge: Harvard University Press, 1988); Jacob Black-Michaud, *Cohesive Forces: Feud in the Mediterranean and the Middle East* (Oxford: Basil Blackwell, 1975); and Franco Ferracuti, Renato Lazzari, and Marvin E. Wolfgang, eds., *Violence in Sardinia* (Rome: Mario Bulzoni, Editore, 1970).

14. *Territory of Arizona v. S. J. 55.*

15. Prison Register no. 3644, Territorial Prison at Florence, Arizona Prison, RG 85, Arizona State Archives, Phoenix.

16. Proclamation of Pardon by Governor Thomas Edward Campbell, August 29, 1917, Arizona Prison, RG 85, Arizona State Archives, Phoenix.

17. In California, death rates for Native American inmates convicted of murder or manslaughter reached 44 percent. Most of them expired within four years. See McKanna, *Race and Homicide,* 99–100.

18. Without medical case files it is impossible to adequately explain this dramatic death rate. For some observations on Native American deaths in California, see Sherburne Cook, *The Population of the California Indians, 1769–1870* (Berkeley: University of California Press, 1976), 104–42. See also McKanna, *Race and Homicide,* 100.

19. Register numbers for the prisoner were Natsin, 698; Batdish, 699; Bakelcle, 700; and Guadalupe, 701. Prison Registers, 1880–1912, Arizona Prison, RG 85, Arizona State Archives, Phoenix.

20. See Proclamation of Pardon, Territory of Arizona, Executive Department, November 28, 1894, ibid.

21. See Proclamation of Pardon by Governor Myron McCord, Territory of Arizona, Executive Department, October 5, 1897, ibid.

22. Register of Prisoners and Index, Ohio State Penitentiary, 355–56.

23. *Arizona Silver Belt,* November 2, 1889.

24. Ibid., December 28, 1889.

25. Ibid.

26. Hayes, *Apache Vengeance,* 126.

27. Gonshayee had attempted suicide after his first trial and conviction before the U.S. District Court in Phoenix, Arizona. A newspaper reporter claimed that Gonshayee, while being held by the U.S. marshal in Phoenix "under sentence of death, attempted to take his own life in the county jail this morning. About 9 o'clock the attention of the prisoners was attracted to the cell occupied by the condemned by a strange noise as though some one was strangling. Burns, a prisoner, proceeded to investigate and found that the Indian had spliced a couple small pieces of rope together, and tying one end about his neck and the other a bar of the cage, was suspended, and would soon have died but for the timely interference of Burns." *Arizona Champion,* June 23, 1888; and *Arizona Silver Belt,* June 23, 1888.

28. *Arizona Weekly Enterprise,* December 7, 1889.

29. See *Arizona Weekly Enterprise,* October 19 and 26, November 16, and December 7, 1889; *Arizona Silver Belt,* November 2, 1889; and *San Francisco Examiner,* December 7, 1889. See also the *Arizona Champion,* June 18, 1887. In an editorial on the impending executions, the *Arizona Champion* noted, "Florence will soon have a hanging picnic of five Apaches. . . . A step in the right direction. If the civil authorities had dealt with these 'Red Devils' all along since Arizona became a Territory, the Apache troubles would have been quelled long before they were." October 26, 1889.

30. Dozens of twentieth-century novels have turned the Apache into the perfect "red devil" villain. See Sonnichsen, "Ambivalent Apache," 99–114. In his discussion of the vilification of Apaches in modern fiction, Sonnichsen observes that "the Enemy must be totally bad. No redeeming features are possible." Ibid., 107.

31. As quoted in an editorial essay by Charles L. Lindner, "A Study of Diverging Careers in the Geronimo Pratt Case," *Los Angeles Times,* February 28, 1999.

32. Harring, *White Man's Law,* 241–50; Karsten, *Between Law and Custom,* 112–14.

33. See photograph of Gonshayee and four other Apaches, AHS no. 30415 (courtesy of Arizona Historical Society, Tucson).

34. Donald Black, *Sociological Justice* (New York: Oxford University Press, 1989), 58–61.

35. *New York Times,* September 4, 1892, and November 20, 1892.

SELECTED BIBLIOGRAPHY

ARCHIVAL SOURCES

Bureau of Indian Affairs. *Annual Report of the Commissioner of Indian Affairs, 1880–1890*. Washington, D.C.: Government Printing Office.

————. *Annual Report of the Commissioner of Indian Affairs to the Secretary of the Interior, 1880–1909*. Washington, D.C.: Government Printing Office.

General Court Martial of First Sergeant Kid, Company A, Indian Scouts. Judge Advocate General, Records Received, 4475, December 27, 1887. National Archives, Washington, D.C.

Pinal County District Court, Case Files 15, 24, and 35, October 1889. RG 111. Arizona State Archives, Phoenix.

Prison Registers, 1880–1912, Arizona Prison. RG 85. Arizona State Archives, Phoenix.

Register of Prisoners and Index, Vol. 14, December 1886–February 1889, Ohio State Penitentiary, Columbus. Ohio State Historical Society.

Registers of Criminal Action and Criminal Case Files, 1880–1920, Globe, Gila County. RG 103. Arizona State Archives, Phoenix.

Report of Committees of the House of Representatives, 1885–1886. Washington, D.C.: Government Printing Office, 1886.

Revised Statutes of the United States, 1873–1874. Washington, D.C.: Government Printing Office, 1875.

San Carlos Agency. Detachment of Indian Scouts, July 19, 1892. Box 12, F, no. 187, MS-707. Arizona Historical Society, Tucson.

Secretary of the Interior. *Annual Report of the Secretary of the Interior, 1880–1890.* Washington, D.C.: Government Printing Office.

Statutes at Large of the United Sates, 1907–1909. Washington, D.C.: Government Printing Office, 1909.

Statutes at Large of the United States of America, 1883–1885. Washington, D.C.: Government Printing Office, 1885.

COURT CASES

Ex Parte Captain Jack, 130 U.S. 354 (1889).

Ex Parte Crow Dog, 109 U.S. 556–572 (1883).

Ex Parte Gonshayee, 130 U.S. 344 (1889).

People v. C. W. Myers, 70 Cal 583 (1886).

People v. Dick, 32 Cal 213 (1867).

People v. E. P. McCurdy, 68 Cal 582–83 (1886).

People v. Shuler, 28 Cal 490 (1865).

People v. Strong, 30 Cal 151 (1866).

Territory of Arizona v. Batdish, Bakelcle, Guadalupe, and Natsin, U.S. District Court, Second Judicial District, Gila County, Arizona Territory, October 26, 1890.

Territory of Arizona v. Batdish, Bakelcle, Natsin, and Guadalupe, 1891, Case no. 67, Supreme Court of the Territory of Arizona, January 8, 1891.

Territory of Arizona v. Captain Jack, Case no. 117, U.S. District Court, Second Judicial District, Gila County, Arizona Territory, October 28, 1889.

Territory of Arizona v. Nahdeizaz, Case no. 113, U.S. District Court, Second Judicial District, Gila County, Arizona Territory, October 23, 1889.

Territory of Arizona v. S. J. 55, U.S. District Court, Fifth Judicial District, Gila County, Arizona Prison.

U.S. v. Captain Jack, U.S. District Court, Second Judicial District, Phoenix, Maricopa County, Arizona Territory, 1888.

U.S. v. Gonshayee, U.S. District Court, Second Judicial District, Phoenix, Maricopa County, Arizona Territory, June 4, 1888.

U.S. v. Kagama, 118 U.S. 375–85 (1886).

U.S. v. Nahdeizaz, U.S. District Court, Second Judicial District, Phoenix, Maricopa County, Arizona Territory, May 11, 1887.

U.S. v. Sayes, U.S. District Court, Second Judicial District, Phoenix, Maricopa County, Arizona Territory.

NEWSPAPERS

(Florence) *Arizona Weekly Enterprise*
(Globe) *Arizona Silver Belt*
New York Times
(Prescott) *Arizona Champion*
(Tucson) *Arizona Weekly Citizen*

SECONDARY SOURCES

Ahearn, Wilbert H. "Assimilationist Racism: The Case of the 'Friends of the Indian.'" *Journal of Ethnic Studies* 4 (Summer 1976): 23–32.

Bakken, Gordon Morris. *Practicing Law in Frontier California.* Lincoln: University of Nebraska Press, 1991.

Ball, Eve. *Indeh: An Apache Odyssey.* Provo, Utah: Brigham Young University Press, 1980.

Bender, Averam B. *A Study of Western Apache Indians, 1846–1886.* New York: Garland, 1974.

Bessler, John D. *Legacy of Violence: Lynch Mobs and Executions in Minnesota.* Minneapolis: University of Minnesota Press, 1993.

Betzinez, Jason. *I Fought with Geronimo.* Harrisburg, Pa.: Stackpole, 1959.

Bourke, John G. "Distillation by Early American Indians." *American Anthropologist* 7 (July 1894): 297.

———. "Medicine-Men of the Apache." *Ninth Annual Report of the*

214 SELECTED BIBLIOGRAPHY

Bureau of Ethnology Washington, D.C.: U.S. Government Printing Office, 1892.

Boyer, L. Bryce. *Childhood and Folklore: A Psychoanalytic Study of Apache Personality.* New York: Library of Psychological Anthropology, 1979.

Braatz, Timothy. *Surviving Conquest: A History of the Yavapai Peoples.* Lincoln: University of Nebraska Press, 2003.

Chapman, Daniel T. "The Great White Father's Little Red Indian School." *American Heritage: The Magazine of History* 22 (December 1970): 48–50.

Chomsky, Carol. "The United States–Dakota War Trials: A Study of Military Injustice." *Stanford Law Review* 43 (November 1990): 17.

Clum, Woodworth. *Apache Agent: The Story of John P. Clum.* Lincoln: University of Nebraska Press, 1978.

Coleman, Michael C. *American Indian Children at School, 1850–1930.* Jackson: University Press of Mississippi, 1993.

Cremony, John C. *Life Among the Apaches.* Lincoln: University of Nebraska Press, 1983.

Davis, Britton. *The Truth about Geronimo.* New Haven: Yale University Press, 1929.

Eastman, Elaine Goodale. *Pratt: The Red Man's Moses.* Norman: University of Oklahoma Press, 1935.

Fear-Segal, Jacqueline. "Nineteenth-Century Indian Education: Universalism Versus Evolutionism." *Journal of American Studies* 33, no. 2 (1999): 328.

Friedman, Lawrence M., and Robert V. Percival. *The Roots of Justice: Crime and Punishment in Alameda County, California, 1870–1910.* Chapel Hill: University of North Carolina Press, 1981.

Goodwin, Grenville. *The Social Organization of the Western Apache.* Chicago: The University of Chicago Press, 1942.

———. *Western Apache Raiding & Warfare: From the Notes of Grenville Goodwin.* Edited by Keith H. Basso. Tucson: University of Arizona Press, 1971.

Greenfeld, Philip J. "Escape from Albuquerque: An Apache Memorate." *American Indian Culture and Research Journal* 25, no. 3 (2001): 47–71.

Hamilton, Allan McL. "The Scientific Detection of Crime." *Appletons' Journal of Literature, Science, and Art* 15 (June 24, 1876): 826.

Harring, Sidney L. *Crow Dog's Case: American Indian Sovereignty, Tribal Law, and United States Law in the Nineteenth Century.* Cambridge, UK: Cambridge University Press, 1994.

———. *White Man's Law: Native People in Nineteenth-Century Canadian Jurisprudence.* Toronto: University of Toronto Press, 1998.

Hayes, Jess G. *Apache Vengeance: True Story of Apache Kid.* Albuquerque: University of New Mexico Press, 1954.

Hietter, Paul T. "How Wild Was Arizona? An Examination of Pima County's Criminal Court, 1882–1909." *Western Legal History* 12 (Summer/Fall 1999): 183–210.

Hoebel, E. Adamson. *The Law of Primitive Man: A Study in Comparative Legal Dynamics.* New York: Atheneum, 1970.

Holmes, Oliver Wendell. "Law in Science and Science in Law," *Harvard Law Review* 12 (1899): 237–38.

Karsten, Peter. *Between Law and Custom: "High" and "Low" Legal Cultures in the Lands of the British Diaspora—The United States, Canada, Australia, and New Zealand, 1600–1900.* Cambridge, UK: Cambridge University Press, 2002

Kawashima, Yasuhide. *Puritan Justice and the Indian: White Man's Law in Massachusetts.* Middletown, Conn.: Wesleyan University Press, 1986.

Llewellyn, K. N., and E. Adamson Hoebel. *Cheyenne Way: Conflict and Case Law in Primitive Jurisprudence.* Norman: University of Oklahoma Press, 1941.

Lockwood, Frank C. *The Apache Indians.* Lincoln: University of Nebraska Press, 1987.

McKanna, Clare V., Jr. *Homicide, Race, and Justice in the American West, 1880–1920.* Tucson: University of Arizona Press, 1997.

————. "Life Hangs in the Balance: The U.S. Supreme Court's Review of *Ex Parte Gonshayee*." *Western Legal History* 3 (Summer/Fall 1990): 197–211.

————. "Murderers All: The Treatment of Indian Defendants in Arizona Territory, 1880–1912." *American Indian Quarterly* 17 (Summer 1993): 359–69.

————. *Race and Homicide in Nineteenth-Century California*. Reno: University of Nevada Press, 2002.

————. *The Trial of "Indian Joe": Race and Justice in the Nineteenth-Century West*. Lincoln: University of Nebraska Press, 2003.

Meriam, Lewis. *The Problem of Indian Administration*. New York: Johnson Reprint, 1971.

Meyer, Roy W. *History of the Santee Sioux: United States Indian Policy on Trial*. Lincoln: University of Nebraska Press, 1993.

Moriarity, Cecil C. H. "Taking of Cast of Footprints." *Police Journal* 5 (1932): 229–32.

Morland, Nigel. *An Outline of Scientific Criminology*. New York: Philosophical Library, 1950.

Newton, Nell Jessup. "Federal Power over Indians: Its Sources, Scope, and Limitation." *University of Pennsylvania Law Review* 132 (January 1984): 212–18.

Opler, Morris Edward. *An Apache Life-Way: The Economic, Social, and Religious Institutions of the Chiricahua Indians*. Lincoln: University of Nebraska Press, 1996.

Powers, Edwin. *Crime and Punishment in Early Massachusetts, 1620–1692: A Documentary History*. Boston: Beacon Press, 1966.

Pratt, Richard Henry. *Battlefield and Classroom: Four Decades with the American Indian, 1867–1904*. Edited by Robert M. Utley. Lincoln: University of Nebraska Press, 1987.

Reece, R. H. W. *Aborigines and Colonists: Aborigines and Colonial Society in New South Wales in the 1830s and 1840s*. Sydney: Sydney University Press, 1974.

Reid, John Phillip. *A Law of Blood: The Primitive Law of the Cherokee Nation*. New York: New York University Press, 1970.

Robinson, Charles M., III, ed. *The Diaries of John Gregory Bourke, Volume 1: November 20, 1872–July 28, 1876.* Denton: University of North Texas Press, 2003.

Rubenstein, Bruce. "To Destroy a Culture: Indian Education in Michigan, 1855–1900." *Michigan History* 60 (Summer 1976): 151–60.

Schmitt, Martin F., ed. *General George Crook: His Autobiography.* Norman: University of Oklahoma Press, 1960.

Smith, Sherry L. *The View from Officers' Row: Army Perception of Western Indians.* Tucson: University of Arizona Press, 1990.

Sonnichsen, C. L. "The Ambivalent Apache." *Western American Literature* 10 (Summer 1975): 99–114.

Stockel, H. Henrietta. *Survival of the Spirit: Chiricahua Apaches in Captivity.* Reno: University of Nevada Press, 1993.

Tate, Michael. "'Pershing's Pets': Apache Scouts in the Mexican Punitive Expedition of 1916." *New Mexico Historical Review* 66, no. 1 (1991): 57–58.

Taylor, Alfred Swaine. *A Manual of Medical Jurisprudence.* Philadelphia: Henry C. Lea, 1866.

———. *Principles and Practices of Medical Jurisprudence.* London: Churchill Livingstone, 1865.

Thrapp, Dan L. *Al Sieber: Chief of Scouts.* Norman: University of Oklahoma Press, 1964.

———. *The Conquest of Apacheria.* Norman: University of Oklahoma Press, 1967.

Utley, Robert M. "The Ordeal of Plenty Horses." *American Heritage: The Magazine of History* 36 (December 1974).

Wellman, Paul I. *Death in the Desert: The Fifty Years' War for the Great Southwest.* Lincoln: University of Nebraska Press, 1935.

Wharfield, H. B. *Apache Indian Scouts.* El Cajon, Calif.: n.p., 1964.

———. "Footnotes to History: Apache Kid and the Record." *Journal of Arizona History* 6 (January 1965): 39.

INDEX